Simple and Practical

Costing, Pricing and Credit Control

How to Improve Profitability
How to Get Paid Promptly

Keith Kirkland and Stuart Howard

KOGAN PAGE

First published in 1998

Kogan Page Limited
120 Pentonville Road
London N1 9JN

Illustrations by John Loader

British Library Cataloguing in Publication Data

A CIP record for this book is available from the British Library

ISBN 0 7494 2930 5

Typeset by Vector Business Development.
Printed and bound in Great Britain by Bell & Bain Ltd, Glasgow.

Contents

Chapter 1

Introduction

Three factors affect business profitability; these are price, volumes and cost. Unfortunately, each affects the other; price affects volume, volume affects cost, and cost affects price. Getting all three right is a delicate balancing act. In this book, we will look at various methods of setting prices, calculating costs, and estimating sales volumes.

Price is hard to determine because finding the 'ideal' price is so difficult. Customers don't just buy on price. They are influenced by all sorts of intangibles like advertising, promotion, image, fashion, 'hype', perceived quality etc. This is why it is almost impossible to determine the 'ideal' price. How high can you go? Cynics say that there are only three areas where there is no price ceiling – fast horses, fast cars and fast women!

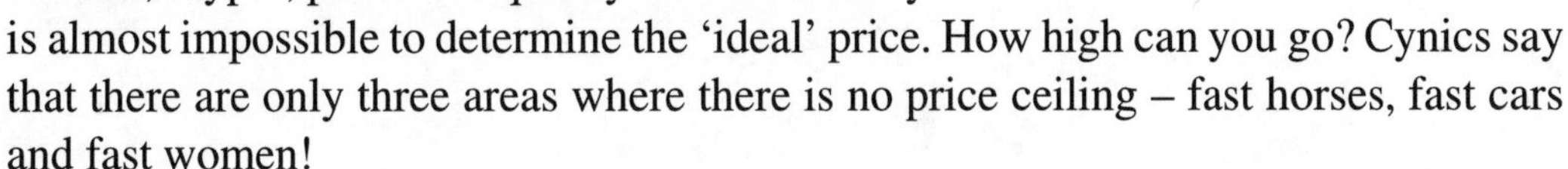

Costing is fascinating – this workbook introduces four methods. We need to understand costs in order to control them. Effective cost control can mean the difference between profit and loss for many businesses.

Many businessmen have difficulty pricing their product or service so they, effectively, allow their competitors to dictate price. In doing this, they may be missing out on a great opportunity to generate additional profits from an understanding of what makes the business really tick.

Chapter 2

Pricing a Product

It is important to set the right price. Here's an example of how a small change in price can produce a big change in profitability.

Example 1

Suppose a greengrocer normally sells £10,000 of apples. What would happen to the profit if:

- he raised apple prices by 1% (ie 1p in the £) ***and still sold the same weight of apples,*** or
- he lowered apple prices by 1% ***and still sold the same weight of apples.***

Let's work out the effect on profits resulting from these price changes.

	Before	After 1% price rise	After 1% price cut
Value of Sales (£)	10,000	10,100	9,900
Total Costs (£)	8,000	8,000	8,000
Profit (£)	2,000	2,100	1,900
% Change in Profit	–	+5%	-5%

These figures show that a 2% change in price can produce a 10% change in profits.

Note: To keep the arithmetic simple, we have priced the apples in the cartoon at 99p per kilo and £1.01 per kilo. In practice, of course, some people will buy apples at 99p per kilo whereas they may not buy at £1.01 per kilo. This is because the price crosses the psychological barrier of £1 per kilo. However, don't let the desire to keep the arithmetic simple confuse the message which is 'small changes in price can produce big changes in profit'.

Exercise 1

Using the same figures as the example above, work out what would be the effect of a 5% change in price assuming that there was no change in the weight of apples sold.

Compare your answer with the model on page 147.

Setting prices can be more of an art than a science. The 'right' price has to satisfy both buyer and seller. On the one hand, the price can't be so low that the seller makes no profit. On the other hand, the price can't be so high that it frightens customers away. Between these two extremes, there is a whole range of possible prices.

In theory, the higher the price, the less the customer buys. This is because, at higher prices, increasing numbers of customers decide that the product fails to satisfy their sense of value.

In practice, pricing a product can be complicated. Many factors affect the customer's decision to buy. Some customers buy on impulse without even giving price a thought! Ideally, we would like to experiment with different prices so that we can check customers' reactions at different price levels. However, it is hard to experiment with price because you upset customers who hear of others paying a lower price.

The diagram below shows a classic price/demand curve. Demand is the amount that customers want to buy at any particular price. If the product were only sensitive to price, and no other factors were involved, you would see the relationship between price and customer demand shown in the graph below.

The graph is marked with:

- the price ceiling – this price is so high that nobody in their right mind will buy.
- the price floor – this is the lowest price that the seller can make a profit. Below this price, it is uneconomic for the seller to supply the market.

'Classic' Price/Demand Curve

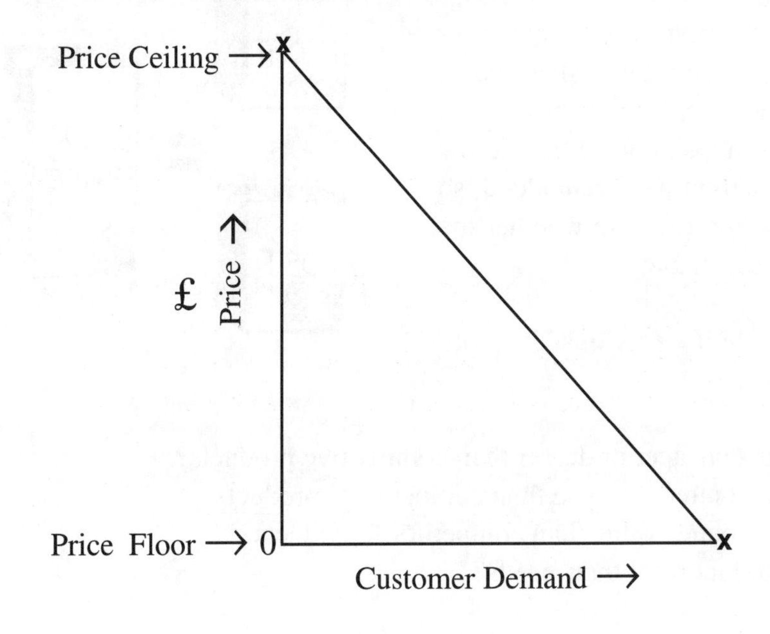

In the real world, of course, higher price doesn't always mean lower sales. For example, the purchase of an engagement ring may celebrate a joyous occasion when people spend as much as they can afford. In this case, the higher priced item could be more attractive.

Essential items, like basic foodstuffs, have to be bought, irrespective of price. If there are shortages of food (as in wartime), people still have to buy food even if the price is higher than they would normally pay.

Too low a price can also be a problem. Too low a price could give the impression that the article lacks quality. Perversely, this could mean that a drop in price leads to a drop in sales!

Pricing

Many businesses set their price by adding a profit margin to cost. Despite the widespread use of this method, 'cost plus profit pricing' is unlikely to give the best price for the seller (or for the buyer), except by chance. For a start, most customers don't know how much the product cost to make, nor do they know how much profit margin has been added, so they are in no position to judge whether the price is 'fair' or 'reasonable'.

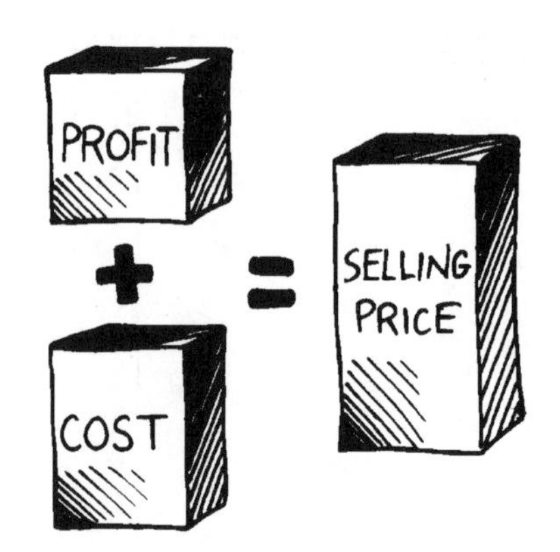

Customers make their decisions on more varied grounds such as:

- Is this product cheaper or dearer than competitive products?
- Is the product better or worse than competitors' products?
- Is the product better value than competitors' products?
- Does this product meet their needs?

- Does it offer value for money?
- How good is it - the perceived quality?
- Will it 'do the job'?
- How much they can afford (either now when the bill has to be paid, or on monthly credit).
- Advertising, branding, image.
- Convenience.
- How much do they trust the supplier.
- Availability.
- How much they *need* it.
- How much they *want* it.

An acceptable price will depend more on the customer's perception of worth rather than product cost.

We have said that the price must be right for the customer but it is also important that the price is right for the seller. Businesses have different targets at different times. For example, the business may be looking to:

- maximise short term profit
- maximise long term profit
- increase market penetration
- have a high rate of growth.

Price will have an important influence on whether the business can reach these targets. For example, a business looking for rapid growth may choose to offer low prices on the basis that low price encourages more people to buy. However, this argument can be a double-edged sword. Sometimes, businesses ask low prices because they fear they may not attract enough customers. This is dangerous especially if prices are set so low that they generate insufficient profits. The resulting strain on finance may be more than the firm can bear. If successful, low prices could attract sufficient customers to overstretch finances to breaking point. This is called overtrading. In extreme cases, it can lead to bankruptcy.

Of course, everyone wants a lot of customers at high profit margins; however, this rarely happens. Which symbols would you put in the boxes in the following diagram?

Exercise 2

Which symbols would you put in the boxes in the diagram following?

	Low Sales	High Sales
High Profit Margin	High Profit Margin Few Sales	High Profit Margin Many Sales
Low Profit Margin	Low Profit Margin Few Sales	Low Profit Margin Many Sales

Compare your answer with the model on page 147.

Practical Price Setting Techniques

If high prices really do discourage customers from buying, and low prices encourage them to buy, then the price should be decided by customer reaction. From a pricing standpoint, we can identify three situations. We need to 'pitch' for the middle one.

- The price is too high (you lose both custom and profit).
- The price is 'right' (the customer is prepared to pay that price but no more).
- The price is too low (you sell a lot of product for little profit).

Here are some steps which you can take to check whether the price is 'right'.

- Ask customers what they think of your prices. Either do it yourself or pay someone else to do it on your behalf.
- Watch customers' reactions when they pick up your product and see the price (or read your price list, or read the price on your estimate etc).
- Study their reactions when you tell them the price. Was their pained expression genuine . . . or fake?
- Find out why customers buy your product/ service. Find out why they choose a particular supplier. Price is only *one* of the factors customers consider when making a buying decision. Is it the most important factor for your customers?
- Find out how customers rate your products/services against your competitors'.

Watch customers' reactions when they see your price

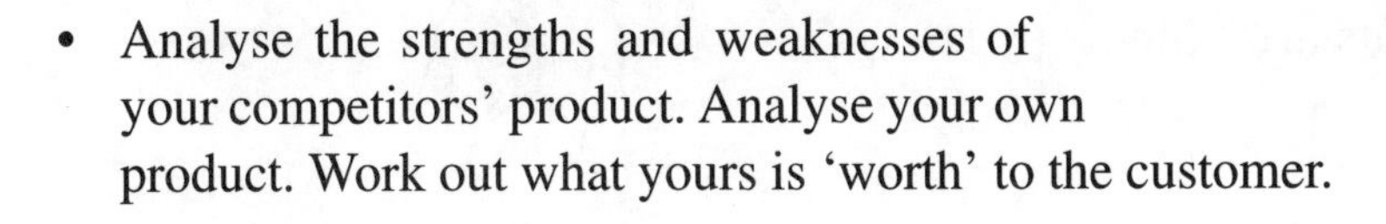

- Analyse the strengths and weaknesses of your competitors' product. Analyse your own product. Work out what yours is 'worth' to the customer.

- Get competitors' prices/quotes. Find out if they will negotiate on price, credit or discounts.
- Get competitors' brochures, prices lists, exhibition catalogues, adverts etc.
- Enlist the help of all your staff who come into contact with customers. Don't take hearsay at face value. Record your findings and make use of them.
- Quote different prices to different people but beware of upsetting them. Also beware of drawing conclusions from different groups of people. Their opinions may not be comparable.
- If in doubt, start with a high price and steadily reduce it, if necessary.

How to Present your Price so Customers say 'Yes'

We have seen that modest increases in price can lead to significant increases in profit. This means that it is important to justify your price to your customers. Here are thirty tried and tested ways of getting a higher price.

- **Sell to the easier parts of the market, where they:**
  – buy from habit
  – have greater desire
  – can afford it
  – don't know other prices.

- **Develop a 'USP' (Unique Selling Proposition)**
  Be better – then you don't have so many close competitors.
  Special benefits merit higher prices.

- **Sell to your existing customers:**
  – sell more of the same
  – sell related items
  – sell them an up-market version
  – ask them what other things they would like to buy.

- **Sell to the rich.**
  Boost the quality. Sell them the best.

- **Sell to the 'MAN'** (The people with the Money, Authority, Need)
  Where the 'MAN' is three different people, start with the one who needs it badly, but doesn't have to pay.

- **Add value and better services.**

- **Build desire before you tell them the price.**

- **Compare yourself with higher priced competitors.**
  Not lower priced ones.

- **Tell them it's their last chance.**
  For example, before you sell out, or before the price goes up.

- **Condition them to think it will be high.**
  Surround it with opulence.

- **Sell them on the idea of 'value for money' instead of price.**
  Focus on the value rather than the money.

- **Give something free with it.**

- **Present the price in a quietly confident way.**
  Professional buyers are paid to give sellers a hard time on price. Some buyers bully sellers who seem nervous or unsure.

Give something free with it

- **Give a concession.**
  Make them think they've won.

- **Explain what they get for their money.**
  Concentrate on those benefits that match their needs.

- **Make buying a comfortable and pleasant experience.**

- **Make buying exciting.**

- **Put it into perspective.**
  How can they argue over the price of a 50p pair of shoelaces when they've just spent £50 on the pair of shoes?

- **'Fly a kite'.**
  Ask for more to begin with; then the true price is a pleasant surprise.

- **Take away the risk.**
  Many buyers pay more for peace of mind. Find out what worries them. Prove to them that you have the solution. Charge them more. And never, ever let them down.

- **Show them it's a bargain.**

- **Break down the price.**
  If it's £50 more than a competitor charges, that's less than £l a week for a year. £10 more per metre is only 10p more per centimetre, or 1p more per millimetre.

- **Tell them how good a track record you've got.**
  Tell them about your famous customers, or quote testimonials.

- **Sell to people who have fewer alternative suppliers to choose from.**

- **Become their sole supplier.**

- **Sell to 'trendsetters'.**
  They'll pay more to be first.

- **Get the endorsement of a famous name.**
  For example, designer label products.

- **Offer credit.**
  Make it easy to pay. Make it affordable.

- **Produce a 'flagship'.**
  Offer a product/service which is superb and desirable but very highly priced. It doesn't matter too much if you don't sell many because, relative to that, your other prices will seem reasonable. Value is relative.

- **Get them to like you and trust you.**
  We prefer to buy from people we like and trust, and we'll pay a little more for the privilege.

And here's 10% more. Free! . . .

- **Improve the product/service as you raise the price.**
  'Now...new improved Zappo, with added zvt!!'

- **Don't focus on price in your adverts and brochures (etc).**
  Tell them about quality instead. Then you're likely to attract buyers for whom quality is more important than price.

- **Put your adverts in quality magazines rather than 'freebies'.**
  People judge you by the company that you keep, and expect to pay accordingly.

A Word About Price Discounting

It can be very tempting to discount prices on the assumption that reduced prices will mean increased sales which will, in turn, lead to increased profitability. This is a dangerous practice because discounting can have profound effects on profitability. Please read the chapter on Contribution Theory (Chapter 6) before discounting prices.

Price discounting can hurt!

Chapter 3

Costing a Product

Costs fall into two broad categories. These are:

- Direct Costs and
- Indirect Costs.

Let's have a look at each in a little more detail.

Direct Costs

Direct costs are costs which are *directly* involved in the production of a product. They include parts and materials, manufacturing labour and manufacturing expenses. Some people call direct costs 'prime costs'. Don't let this put you off; direct costs and prime costs are just two different words for the same thing.

There are three basic types of direct costs. These are:

- Direct *Labour* Costs
- Direct *Material* Costs
- Direct *Expense*

Here is an explanation of each type.

Direct Labour

Direct labour is labour which is *directly* associated with producing a product.

Direct Labour

Generally speaking, direct labour personnel handle the product from the time it arrives as raw material to the time it is wrapped in packaging material ready for dispatch.

In labour intensive activities, direct labour costs will obviously be a significant percentage of product cost. In this case, savings on direct labour will be important since every pound taken off cost is a pound added to profit.

Direct Material

Direct materials comprise the materials which are *directly* identified with the job in hand. Direct materials include raw materials, bought in sub-assemblies, components, packaging etc. They can also include carriage inwards and allowances for waste, spillage, spoilage, pilferage etc.

Steel stock is a direct material

Just as in some industries direct labour can account for the majority of the cost, in other industries direct material will be the key factor. This particularly applies where an industry assembles or processes other people's output, eg motor car manufacture, food processing, consumer durables etc. In these industries, intelligent buying of materials has an important influence on cost and hence on business profits.

There are several ways of valuing material stocks. These include:

- First In First Out (FIFO) – in this system, material costs are charged to jobs based on the cost of the oldest material in stock.
- Last In First Out (LIFO) – in this system, costs are charged to jobs based on the cost of the newest material taken into stock.
- Average Cost – the average of all the materials costs in stock.
- Weighted Average – the cost of all materials bought for use. Costs are weighted according to the quantities bought at each price.
- Standard Cost – the cost of the materials which *should* be incorporated into a job according to the standard method of production.

The method of valuing materials is important because:

- It will affect the cost of the job which incorporates that material.
- It will affect the value of the stock left in the stockroom.
- It will affect current operating costs and hence profits reported in the current period.

It is better to decide on a method of stock valuation and stick with it until there is a definite reason to change. In this way, most of the ups and downs of stock valuation cancel themselves out in the longer term.

Where the business is big enough to employ a buyer, all orders should be placed through him or her so as to negotiate the best prices and delivery. Proper controls should exist in ordering, storage, issue and usage of all materials. Slack storekeeping can lead to inaccuracies and losses by theft and neglect. These hidden costs will work through into lost profit for the business.

Direct Expense

'Direct expense' covers any expenditure other than direct labour or direct material which can be traced directly to the job or process. Obvious examples include jigs, tools and production drawings costs. Costs of equipment purchased for a particular product or process should also be borne by the job itself. Any items bought for *general* use will, of course, be capitalised and depreciated as an indirect expense.

Direct Expense

Direct expense would also include hire charges. If a business hires a special tool to perform a job then the cost would be chargeable to that job. Similarly, if someone from outside the company has to be hired on a consultancy basis to help produce the product then the cost would be charged to the job as a direct expense.

Indirect Costs

Not all costs are direct costs. The business also incurs other costs which are called indirect costs. Indirect costs are costs involved with the *administration* of the business. They include items such as:

- salesmen's salaries
- administration costs
- depreciation
- research and development
- advertising and public relations
- rent, business rates.

You will sometimes hear people calling indirect costs 'overhead costs'. Don't worry, 'indirect costs' and 'overheads' mean the same thing. We use the terms interchangeably.

Indirect costs are more related to time rather than the level of business activity. This is because these costs continue even when there is little product being produced.

Overheads don't easily relate to specific products or jobs. Overhead costs, therefore, have to be *allocated* or *apportioned* to products. Overhead costs are *allocated* to a product when there is a clearly identified relationship with that product. Allocation implies a degree of precision. On the other hand, overhead costs are said to be *apportioned* when no obvious relationship exists. Sharing overheads by apportionment is a much more arbitrary process. Because of the nature of overheads, apportionment is much more common than allocation.

It is easy to calculate the total level of overheads incurred by the business. However, it is not easy to find a formula for sharing the overheads over the products produced by that business.

Overheads can be shared over the products using some form of 'recovery rate'. Often the recovery rate is calculated as an uplift on the direct cost. This may, or may not, be a sensible method of overhead recovery according to circumstances in your business. Over the years, some methods have been used more than others. Here are some traditional methods of overhead recovery.

Examples of indirect costs

Material Recovery Rate

Where the greater value of production lies in the materials used, overheads can be allocated in proportion to the material consumed on a job. For example, if the annual cost of materials is £100K and the annual overhead £10K then each job will carry an additional 10% over and above the material costs to provide for overhead recovery.

Labour Recovery Rate

Where labour is the predominating factor, it may make sense to use direct labour instead of direct materials as the basis on which overhead charges are apportioned.

Prime Cost Recovery Rate

Prime costs is another term for total direct cost. In some businesses, overheads could be shared out as an uplift on the prime costs incurred on a product or on a job.

Machine Hour Rate

Today many production processes are heavily dependent on machinery. In these areas, machine hours could form the basis on which to apportion overheads.

Percentage of Selling Price

The price charged for a product should recover all of the costs of producing that product, including indirect costs. You may prefer to share out the indirect costs based on a percentage of the selling price. There is no right or wrong way of sharing overheads. The allocation is always subjective. Whatever method is chosen, some product manager or salesman will find a reason why *his* pet product should carry a lesser share of the overheads compared to all the other products!

Standard Costing

Standard costing is a method of working out how much products *ought* to cost. Once a standard cost has been calculated, a business will normally compare the actual cost of production with the standard cost. Detailed comparison will reveal the reason for the cost divergence. Studying the reasons for cost divergence is called 'variance analysis'.

Standard costing is particularly valuable for a repetitive manufacturing process. Standard cost estimates can be prepared which determine the amount of time, material and expense which *should* be expended on the product.

Variance analysis has advantages in terms of management control. Only significant positive or negative variances are reported. This avoids management having to sift through a mass of cost detail. Once the variances are highlighted by type, eg labour variance, material variance etc, an exercise can be undertaken to establish:

- What went wrong?
- Whose responsibility was it?
- What steps is he/she taking to ensure that future costs will be contained?

Sometimes, of course, the responsibility for a cost increase does not lie within the organisation, eg a fuel price rise. Once alternative fuels have been investigated and discarded, there will be no alternative but to incorporate the increased cost into the standard cost.

Standard costing can involve a lot of calculations!

Chapter 4

Pricing a Service

Increasingly, people in Britain earn a living by performing a service instead of producing a product. People who provide a service are usually selling their time and skills to satisfy their customers' wants.

Many professionals like dentists, engineers and consultants use their time, skill and knowledge to earn a living. This also applies to tradesmen such as carpenters, plumbers and electricians. Even those who produce products without the help of machines (such as wedding cakes, craft furniture, bespoke tailoring) are really performing a specialist service for customers rather than manufacturing goods in the traditional sense.

People who repair things also produce a service. Let's take the garage repair bill shown below as an example of pricing/costing a service. The bill may seem to be largely made up of the cost of the spare parts. However, the real cost of providing the service is contained in the labour cost. Here is an example.

Example 2 A Garage Repair Bill

	£
Parts, filters, oil etc	120.18
Labour	111.00
VAT	40.46
Total	271.64

Where do you think the profit was being made? Look at the following cost breakdown:

	Cost	Mark-up	Price	Gross Profit
	£	%	£	£
Parts	104.50	15	120.18	15.68
Labour	37.00	200	111.00	74.00
				89.68

Although the figures are imaginary, they show that the profit for the garage proprietor is not being made in the area of greatest customer expense.

The reasoning behind this approach to charging is very simple. Ultimately, the charge made to the customer must take account not only of the direct costs of running the business but the overheads and profit as well. There is a limit to the amount that can be added to the bought-in cost of materials. The most you can charge a customer is the price he expects to pay for the parts at recommended retail price. *This means that the labour element must make the major contribution to overhead recovery and profit.*

Here is another example.

Example 3

Let's take the case of a self employed graphics designer operating from a small office whose work involves travelling about 200 miles a week for 40 weeks of the year.

The direct costs of this business will be low compared to the manufacturing industry. For example, materials could comprise paper, pencils, paint, computer supplies etc. Even when these items are charged out to a customer's job, there is little scope for profit since the customer will expect to see the costs of these items shown on his bill at normal retail price.

Overhead costs for this business might comprise:

	£
Rent/rates	2500
Advertising	1000
Telephone	300
Insurance	200
Stationery and Postage	100
Sundries	300
Motoring (200 miles x 40 weeks @ 20p per mile)	1600
Total	6000

Calculating the Labour Charges

What standard of living should our designer aim for? £15,000, £20,000 or £40,000 per annum? Remember, the drawings must not only cover what he has to live on but also tax, national insurance, private medical insurance, pension provision etc. To keep the example going, let's say the designer requires drawings of £20,000 per annum.

How Much Time is Saleable?

Nobody can work for 52 weeks a year. There must be time off for holidays and sickness etc. There will also be productive time lost for other reasons, including:

Marketing Time needs to be spent marketing the business. This will vary greatly from one business to another.

Travelling This is not only a cost, it also reduces effective working time.

Purchasing Time has to be spent searching for products from suppliers, wholesalers etc.

Researching This will include a range of activities such as attending exhibitions, conferences, trade shows, libraries in order to keep up-to-date with development in materials, equipment, techniques etc.

Leisure Nobody can work 100 hours a week. Time has to be allowed for holidays, otherwise family life will suffer.

So what percentage of time can our designer sell? Let's assume he attends work for 40 hours a week. For the purpose of argument, we will take three cases. Let's assume that our designer can sell:

(i) 77% of his time
(ii) 58% of his time
(iii) 48% of his time.

Productive hours would, therefore, be:

(i) 77% x 52 weeks = 40 weeks x 40 hours = 1,600 productive hours
(ii) 58% x 52 weeks = 30 weeks x 40 hours = 1,200 productive hours
(iii) 48% x 52 weeks = 25 weeks x 40 hours = 1,000 productive hours.

What will his rates be?

He is budgeting to earn £26,000 pa (£20,000 'drawings' + £6,000 'overheads')

If he sells 77% of his time, he must earn £650 per week (or £16.25 per hour)
If he sells 58% of his time, he must earn £867 per week (or £21.67 per hour)
If he sells 48% of his time, he must earn £1040 per week (or £26.00 per hour)
Plus VAT, if applicable.

Checking the Market Rates

The above example shows a 'charge out' rate based on reasonable assumptions. The next step is to look at the market place. What are the going rates for this trade or profession? This doesn't mean the wages or salaries paid to the individual but the rates charged out to a third party.

For example, we may find that:

- the garage mechanic is charged at about £40 per hour
- your private physiotherapist will charge about £60 per hour
- your accountant will charge about £100 per hour
- your consultant surgeon will charge upwards of £300 per hour.

A number of factors are involved:

- the rarity value of the skill or service
- the quality of the performance
- the extent to which work can be farmed out to less expensive labour
- the number of ancillary services, receptionists, secretaries, technicians etc supported by the charging service.

If the rate calculated by our designer is less than the market rate, he has two courses of action available. Firstly, he can 'up' his rate to the market rate on the basis that too low a rate could deter as many customers as it encourages. Alternatively, the designer could charge out at the lower rate, at least in the short term, on the basis that he could devote more time to each client and, hopefully, build a client portfolio who could be charged slightly more each year so that, eventually, the designer would develop a large and profitable business.

If the rates calculated for our designer are higher than market rate then there are some serious decisions to make. Can overheads be reduced or, alternatively, can the job be done in less time?

Chapter 5

Break-Even Analysis

In Chapters 2 and 3, we looked at the traditional approach to costing which is based on direct and indirect costs. However, there is an alternative approach. Instead of breaking down costs into direct and indirect costs, we can break them down into fixed and variable costs. This alternative costing system can often reveal more about the business than traditional methods. To understand break-even analysis, we need to begin with an explanation of fixed and variable costs.

Fixed Costs

Fixed costs are costs which tend to remain at the same level, irrespective of the amount of product produced or the amount of service performed. Fixed costs do not move in sympathy with the volume of sales that you make. Fixed costs tend to be time related rather than volume related, examples include:

- rent
- rates
- depreciation
- insurance
- management salaries
- administrative salaries
- lease charges.

If shown graphically, they would appear as shown over the page.

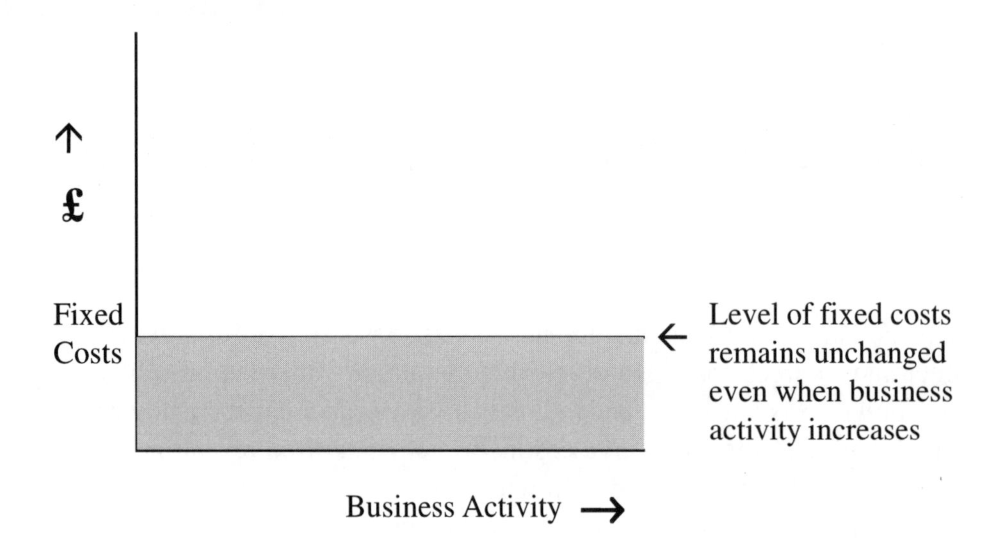

The graph shows that the level of fixed costs remains the same, no matter what the business volume. Business activity (the lower axis) can be measured in a variety of ways. For example, you could have numbers of items sold or value of sales in pounds. You can use whatever measure makes sense.

You will have noticed that many fixed costs are also overhead costs. Don't fall into the trap of assuming that *all* overhead costs are necessarily fixed costs. Whilst it is true that many overhead costs are fixed in nature, you have to be careful because some overheads are variable costs. For example, hire charges may well be shown in the accounts as overheads. However, if equipment has to be hired to meet fluctuations in business activity then they are not fixed costs. In this case, hire charges would be variable costs.

Naturally, no fixed cost is *totally* independent of volume. If volume increases tenfold then additional fixed costs will, obviously, be incurred. Nevertheless, over normal variations in normal business activity, fixed costs should remain stable.

Fixed Costs!

Variable Costs

Variable costs tend to increase in proportion to the amount of goods or services produced. If you draw a graph of variable costs against the level of business activity, it could look something like the illustration below.

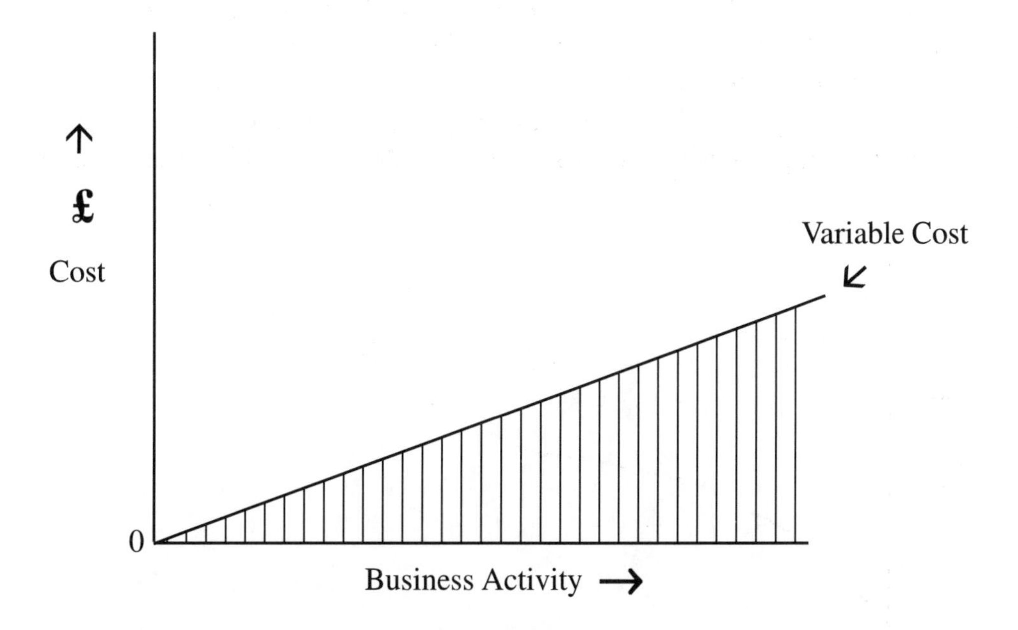

Variable costs usually arise from activities like manufacturing a product, or performing a service. Variable costs include items like casual labour, materials and production expenses.

As you can see, variable costs are often direct costs. However, don't assume all direct costs are automatically variable costs. For example, in many businesses, electricity charges will be classed as overheads. However, in some production processes, increasing levels of production could cause increasing levels of electricity consumption (eg metal smelting). In this case, electricity consumption would be a variable cost.

Semi-Variable Costs

Most costs fall either into the fixed cost category or the variable cost category. However, there are a few costs which are neither truly fixed nor truly variable. These costs are called semi-variable costs.

Semi-variable costs don't meet either the fixed or variable criteria perfectly, they tend to have an element of each. Semi-variable costs will increase with volume although the relationship won't be constant. For example, they may increase over a certain activity range and then remain stable until a trigger point is reached when they will start to rise again. A graph of an imaginary semi-variable cost could appear as follows:

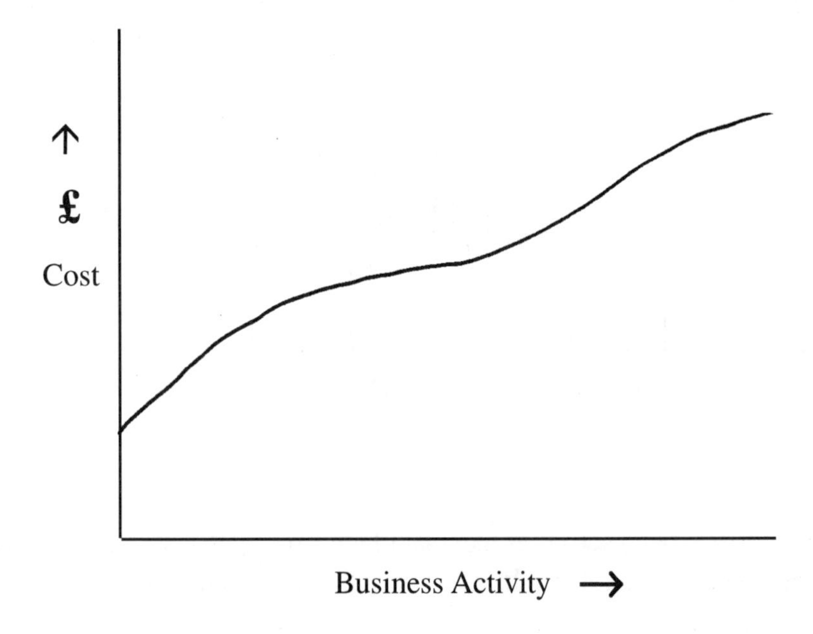

Because of the vague nature of semi-variable costs, no clear relationship normally exists. They are difficult to express graphically. Semi-variable costs may have elements of fixed and variable costs which it is impossible to separate.

Examples of semi-variable cost could include advertising, public relations, cost of computer programming etc.

Fortunately, there are only a few of these problem costs so the solution is usually simple. The answer is to 'force fit' the cost into the fixed or variable category, whichever seems closest. Provided there aren't many of these costs, force fitting them into either fixed costs or variable costs shouldn't produce a significant distortion to the overall result.

Break-Even Charts

It is very revealing to plot on the same graph:

- Fixed costs
- Variable costs
- Sales income.

Here's how to do it. First put the fixed costs onto the graph as follows:

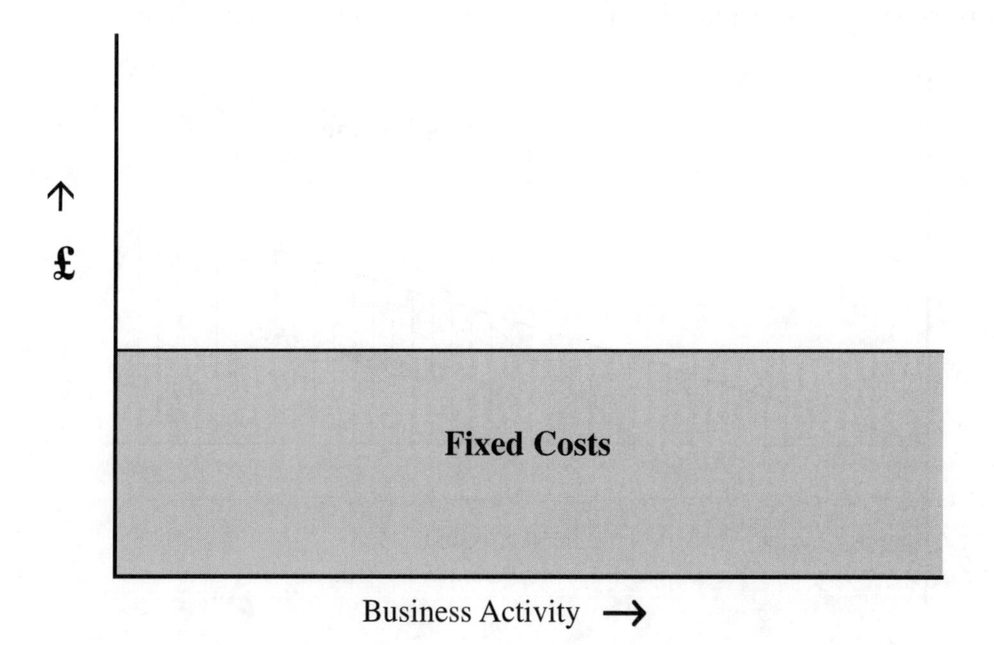

Then add the variable costs line on top of the fixed cost line like so:

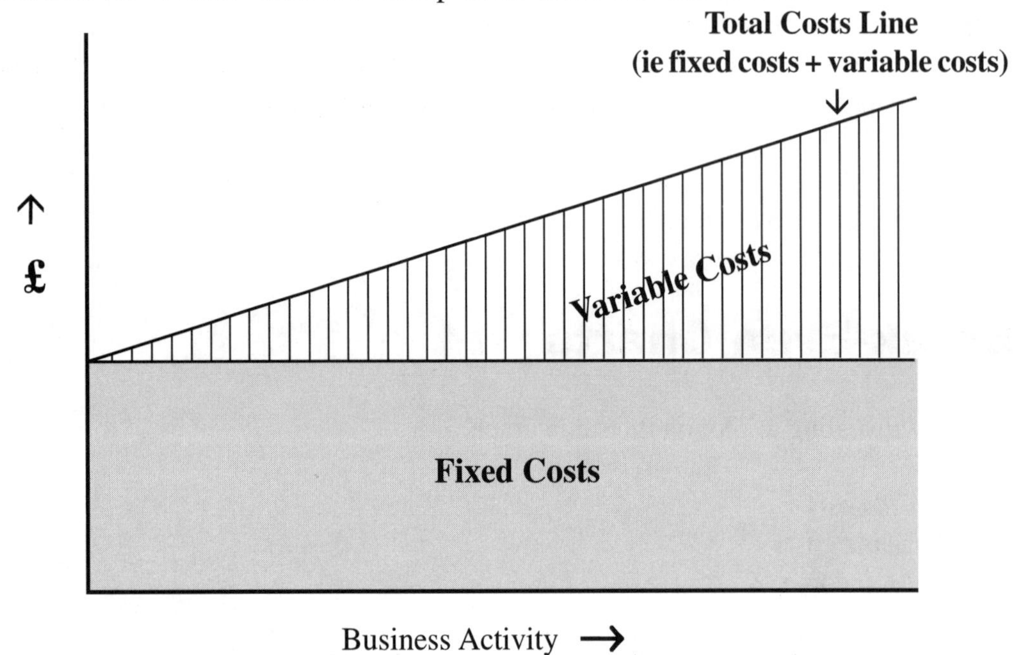

Finally, add the sales income line, making sure the sales line starts at zero.

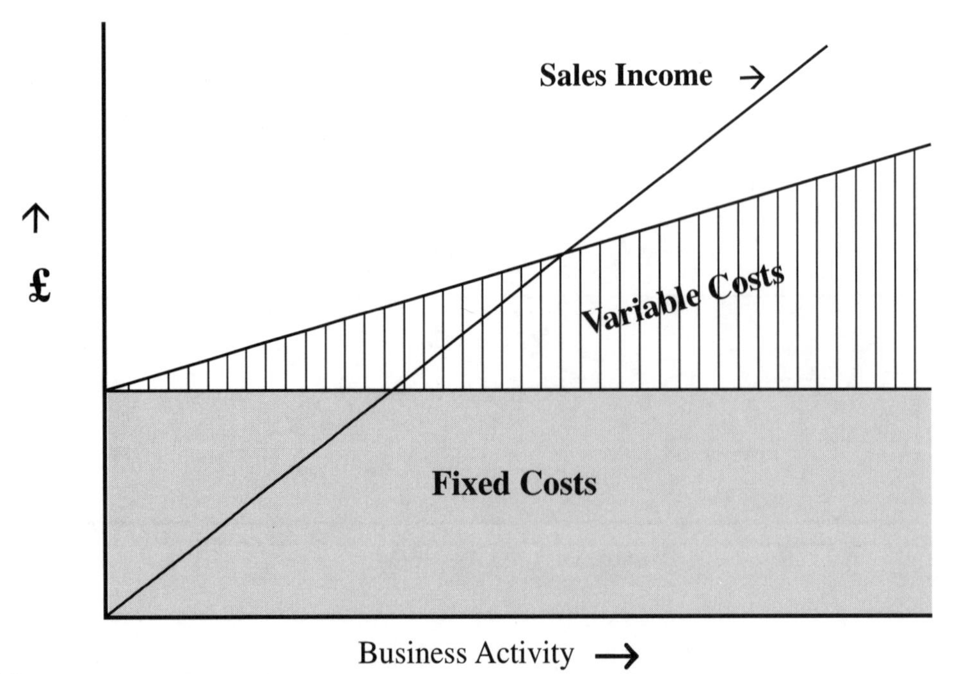

Here are some comments on the graph.

- Note that the fixed cost line is horizontal. Remember, fixed costs remain the same, whatever the level of output (within reason).
- Variable costs increase in proportion to sales. Note that the variable cost line is built *on top of* the fixed cost line. Adding together the 'fixed cost' and 'variable cost' gives the 'total cost' for that level of sales.
- Note that the sales line commences at zero. No sales really does mean no income!

You will notice that there is a point where the sales income line crosses the total costs line. This is called the break-even point. At this point, the business makes neither profit nor loss.

The graph on page 37 shows that, at business activity levels *below* the break-even point, the business makes a loss. At business activity levels *above* the break-even point, the business makes a profit.

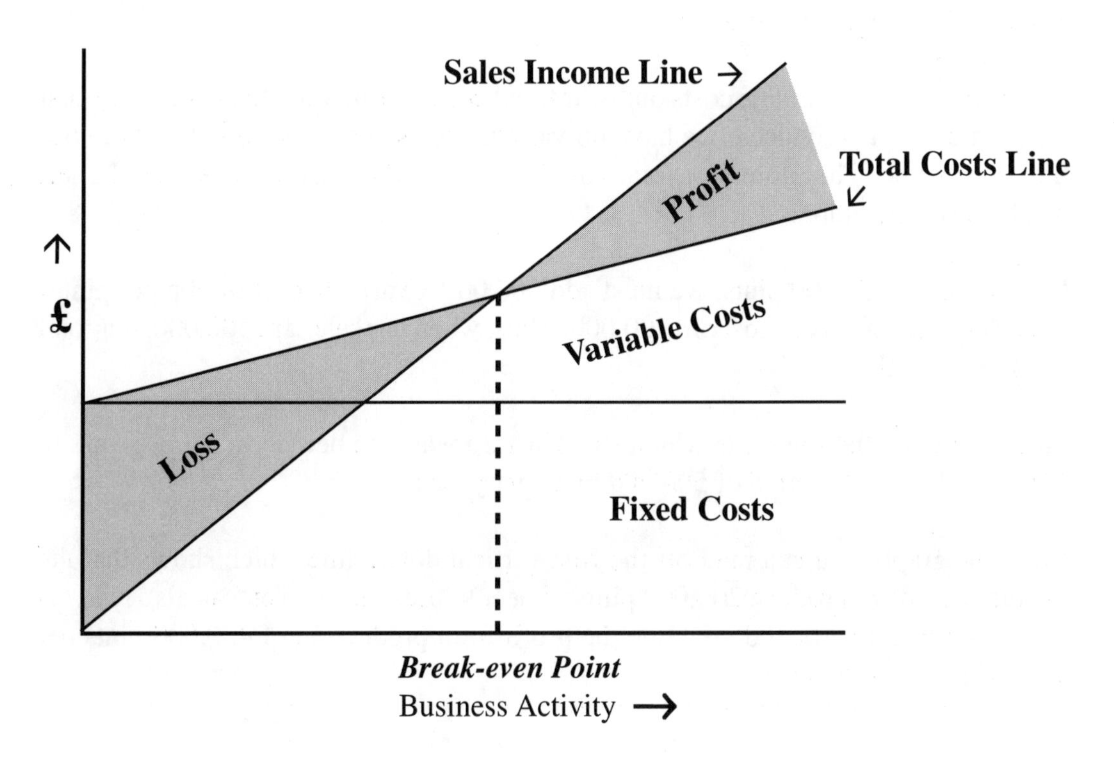

Let's look at a worked example.

Example 4

The Oddfellows Brewery can produce 500,000 pints of beer a year. Costs and selling prices are as follows:

Selling Price	£1 per pint
Variable Cost	50p per pint
Fixed Costs	£100,000 per annum

- How much does the brewery have to sell to break even?
- What profit would be generated if the brewery produced 450,000 pints of beer?

Oddfellows Brewery

The first stage is to draw the fixed costs line. This is a horizontal line drawn across the graph at the £100,000 cost level.

We need to add the variable costs onto our fixed costs line in order to get our total cost line. If no beer is produced, we have no variable costs and so nothing to add to our fixed costs line. Therefore, our total cost line sits on the fixed cost line on the left hand side of the graph.

If we produce 500,000 pints, we must add 500,000 x variable cost of 50p per pint = £250,000 onto our fixed cost of £100,000. Thus, when our sales are 500,000, our total costs are £350,000.

Finally, we add the sales line which starts at zero when no beer is sold and grows to £500,000 for a production of 500,000 pints per year.

From the graph, you can read off the first vertical dotted line which shows that the business needs to produce 200,000 pints of beer to break even. You can also read off from the second vertical dotted line the profit for a production of 450,000 pints per year which is £125,000.

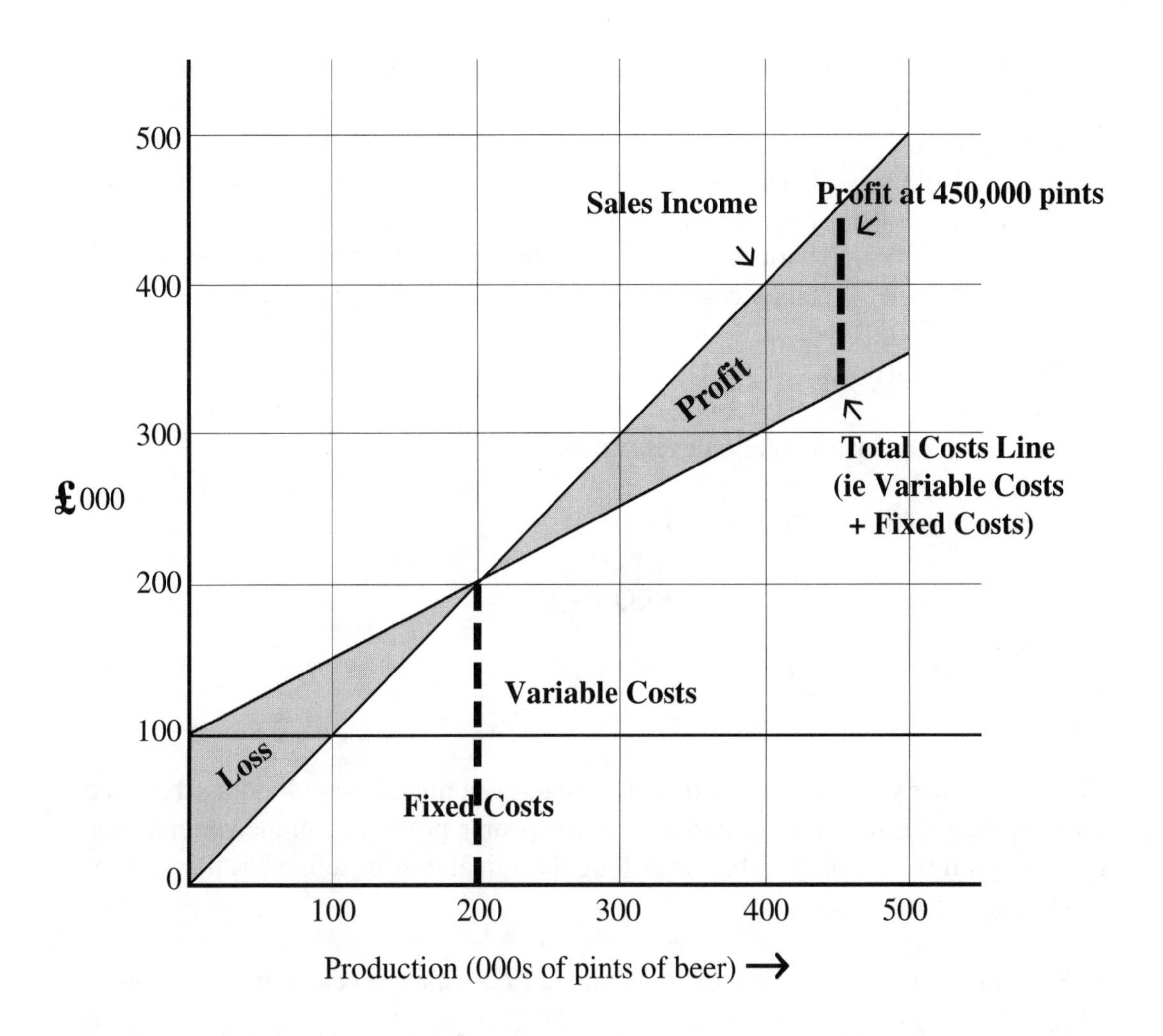

Calculation of the Break-Even Quantity (BEQ)

There is no more fundamental benchmark in business than the dividing line between making a profit and a loss. This dividing line is called the break-even point.

The graph opposite shows the break-even point. This is the point at which the 'sales income' line and the 'total cost' line intersects.

You can work out the break-even quantity without the effort of drawing a graph using the following formula.

Let

Let	BEQ	=	Quantity sold
	P	=	Price per unit
	VC	=	Variable cost per unit (ie cost of producing one more unit)
	F	=	Fixed cost

At the break-even point

Total Cost = Total Sales Revenue

$$F + (BEQ \times VC) = BEQ \times P$$

$$F = (BEQ \times P) - (BEQ \times VC)$$

$$F = BEQ(P - VC)$$

$$BEQ = \frac{F}{P - VC}$$

This shows that you can always find the break-even quantity by dividing the fixed costs by the price less the variable cost. Some people prefer to call the variable cost the 'marginal cost' which is the same thing. Marginal cost is defined as the 'cost of producing one more unit'.

In Example 4, we could have used the formula to calculate break-even as follows:

$$BEQ = \frac{F}{P - VC} = \frac{£100{,}000}{£1 - 50p} = \frac{£100{,}000}{50p}$$

BEQ = 200,000 pints of beer

Exercise 3

You plan to sell ice cream at a carnival. Ice creams can be purchased for 12p each. You can return all those unsold. The rental for the stand at the carnival is £50. Each ice cream will be sold for 22p. There are no other costs.

Calculate:

1 How many ice creams must be sold to break even?

2 How many ice creams must be sold to yield a profit of £20?

Compare your answer with the model on page 148.

A Word of Caution About Break-even Analysis

Break-even analysis tells you a lot about the business. However, you must bear in mind the limitations of the method. These limitations are:

- You must be able to sort costs into fixed costs and variable costs.
- Fixed costs must remain reasonably fixed over the range of output that you are considering.
- Variable costs must increase in sympathy with sales. We have assumed that unit costs remain stable over the range we are considering. Beware if you have dramatic economies of scale when purchasing bought-in materials. This could mean that variable costs per unit decrease as business volumes increase.
- Sales income must increase in proportion to sales. This works fine unless you offer dramatic price discounts to customers in order to achieve higher levels of sales.
- The illustrations that we have used in this section assume that the business produces a single product. We will see in the following sections how to handle businesses which produce a range of products (or perform a variety of services).

Break-even analysis is a great way to understand how price and volume affects business profitability. Used with care, it can be a major benefit in financial decision making.

Chapter 6

Contribution Theory

In Chapter 5, we saw how fixed costs, variable costs and sales volumes are related to each other. We can take this thinking a stage further using something called 'contribution'. Like break-even analysis, contribution uses fixed and variable costs; however, the results are expressed in a slightly different format.

Let's start by defining what we mean by 'contribution'. Contribution is an abbreviation for 'contribution to profit and overhead'. Contribution is the amount left over when you subtract variable costs from selling price. Thus:

	Selling price per unit
less	Variable cost per unit
	Contribution per unit

The amount left over 'contributes' to paying off fixed costs. Any contribution left over after paying off fixed costs is profit for the business.

Look at the example over the page. In this example, a refrigerator manufacturer sells his fridges for £100. The variable cost of making a fridge is £60. This means that the contribution per fridge is £40.

	£
Selling price per fridge	100
Variable cost per fridge	60
Contribution per fridge	40

We can use this information to tell us more about the business.

Example 5

A company makes a refrigerator with a sales price of £100 and a variable cost of £60. Fixed costs are £60,000 per annum. Calculate:

(i) No of units which need to be sold to break even
(ii) No of units which need to be sold to produce a profit of £20,000
(iii) No of units which need to be sold to produce a profit of £200,000.

The contribution per refrigerator is:

		£
	Selling Price	100
less	Marginal Cost	60
	Contribution per fridge	40

(i) Each refrigerator sold contributes £40 to the fixed costs and profits of the firm. If the firm is to reach its break-even point, it only needs to sell enough fridges to recover the fixed costs. Therefore, it must sell:

$$\frac{\text{Fixed Costs}}{\text{Contribution}} = \frac{60000}{40} = 1500 \text{ fridges to break-even}$$

(ii) If the company plans to make a profit of £20,000, it needs to cover its fixed costs *and* generate a further £20,000 profit. We calculated above that it needs to sell 1,500 fridges to break-even. To generate a £20,000 profit, it needs to sell a further:

$$\frac{20000}{40} = 500 \text{ extra fridges to go beyond break-even}$$

Therefore, the manufacturer needs to sell:

$$1500 + 500 = 2000 \text{ fridges to make a profit of £20,000}$$

(iii) To make a profit of £200,000 requires sales of:

$$\frac{60000}{40} = 1500 \text{ fridges to break-even } \textit{plus}$$

$$\frac{200000}{40} = 5000 \text{ fridges to make a profit of £200,000.}$$

Therefore, to make a profit of £200,000, the company needs to sell 6,500 refrigerators.

Here is another example which uses 'contribution' to help reach a decision. In the last example, we looked at contribution for each item sold. In this example, we look at contribution for a whole programme.

Example 6

Superchocs make chocolate bars. They normally make 300,000 bars per month which they sell to the wholesalers for 26p per bar. They have fixed costs of £15,000 per month and variable costs of 15p per bar.

They have been offered an export contract to sell 200,000 chocolate bars for 18p per bar. Should they accept the contract?

Solution

The present financial position is as follows:

		£
	Sales (300,000 x 26p) =	78000
less	Variable Costs (300,000 @ 15p)	45000
	Contribution	33000
less	Fixed Costs	15000
	Net Profit	18000

Providing fixed costs don't change then the export order would produce a further profit of:

		£
	Sales (200,000 x 18p) =	36000
less	Variable Costs (200,000 x 15p)	30000
	Contribution	6000

Notice that we have not charged fixed costs to the export order because they have already been recovered against normal 'home' production. The export order would bring in sales which would be profitable because fixed costs have already been covered. Thus, purely on profit grounds, the order would be acceptable.

However, there are several other factors to be taken into account before a decision is taken.

- Can we get the export customer to pay us more for each chocolate bar?
- Will the low export price make home customers demand lower prices as well?
- Are we sure that fixed costs will not alter?
- Would the special order lock up capacity which could be used for extra home business at better margins?
- Is the export order the most profitable way of using the spare capacity?

Real Life Implication of Contribution Theory

- Any additional business which provides a positive contribution will increase profits (provided fixed costs don't increase).
- Pricing based on variable costs can be used to mop up spare capacity. For example, hotels provide cheap weekend rates, railways and airlines have cheap fares for off-peak periods, many manufacturers of proprietary goods produce lower priced 'own label' products for supermarkets.

- You can't price the *whole* business of a business on a marginal cost basis! The fixed costs have to be recovered somehow.

Exercise 4 Contribution Exercise

Fred operates a road haulage business with one lorry. Fred estimates the running costs of the lorry per quarter are as follows:

Expense	Total for Quarter
	£
Diesel/Oil	1900
Driver's Salary	3750
Tax/Insurance	1200
Servicing/Repairs	500
Depreciation of Vehicle	1500
Total Costs	8850

From the above, he has calculated the average cost per mile as follows:

$$\frac{\text{Total Costs}}{\text{Quarterly Mileage}} = \frac{8850}{40000} = 22.12 \text{ pence per mile}$$

Fred is already meeting his fixed costs out of his existing income. However, he has spare capacity for the lorry for which he wants to secure extra work. He has been asked to bid for a one-off tender. What is the lowest price that Fred could bid per mile and still make a profit? (Assume that all costs are fixed except the cost of diesel/oil and servicing/repairs, both of which depend on the number of miles covered).

Compare your answer with the model on pages 148 and 149.

Limiting Factors

Sometimes, a business may be unable to fulfil its sales orders because of limiting factors like:

- materials shortages
- labour shortages
- insufficient plant capacity
- bottlenecks in key processes.

In these circumstances, the business will want to make best use of the resource in short supply. The following technique illustrates how to schedule production to make the most profit from a temporary shortage. It is stressed that this is only a temporary solution since the long term solution is, of course, to eliminate the limiting factor.

Example 7

Garden Ornaments Ltd manufactures garden gnomes and pools for a variety of retail outlets. Sometimes, they are short of labour; at other times, they are short of materials. Which product should they produce:

(i) when short of labour?
(ii) when short of materials?

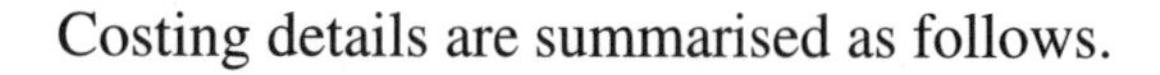

Costing details are summarised as follows.

Garden Gnomes

	£
Selling Price	80
Labour Cost (2 hours)	20
Material Cost (2 bags)	20
Contribution	40

Garden Pools

	£
Selling Price	110
Labour Cost (2 hours)	20
Material Cost (4 bags)	40
Contribution	50

Note: Labour costs £10 per hour
Material comprises sand and cement which costs £10 per bag.

(i) Labour Shortage

Calculate contribution per hour of labour:

Garden Gnomes $\frac{£40}{2 \text{ hrs}}$ = £20 per hour

Garden Pools $\frac{£50}{2 \text{ hrs}}$ = £25 per hour

Conclusion: When labour is in short supply, the firm should produce pools because they offer a greater contribution per unit of labour available.

(ii) Material Shortage

Calculate contribution per bag of material:

Garden Gnomes $\frac{£40}{2 \text{ bags}}$ = £20 per bag

Garden Pools $\frac{£50}{4 \text{ bags}}$ = £12.50 per bag

Conclusion: When material is in short supply, firm should produce garden gnomes because gnomes offer the greatest contribution per unit of material to profit and overheads.

'Make or Buy' Decisions

A business may have a choice whether to manufacture a product entirely by itself or buy parts from outside suppliers. The answer to this 'make or buy' decision will depend on the relative profitability of each course of action.

Example 8

You are currently manufacturing screws for sale. The costs and selling prices for 250 screws are as follows:

Screws (per 250)

		£
	Selling Price	200
less	Marginal Costs	125
	Contribution	75

You can use the same machine to produce bolts. You can produce 1,000 bolts in the time taken to produce 250 screws.

The cost of bolts (per 1,000) is:

	£
Cost from outside supplier	350
Manufacturing costs in-house (incl fixed costs of £160)	400

Would it be more profitable to use your machine to make bolts or screws?

Solution

You are, effectively, trading production of 250 screws against production of 1,000 bolts. You need to work out which course of action will generate the most contribution.

The following information is available.

(i) **Contribution for 1,000 bolts**

		£
	Buying in Price	350
less	Variable Costs (£400 – £160)	240
	Contribution	110

(ii) **Contribution for 250 screws**

		£
	Selling Price	200
less	Marginal Costs	125
	Contribution	75

Therefore, when faced with the choice of making bolts or screws, bolts should always have priority.

Marginal Cost Statements

Marginal cost statements are far more meaningful than normal profit and loss accounts. This is because the separation of costs into fixed and variable costs makes it possible to predict the effect of changes in price, sales volumes, variable costs, fixed costs etc on profit. Many people mistakenly believe that, on a normal profit and loss account, 'cost of sales' will always be variable costs and 'overheads' will always be fixed costs. *This isn't necessarily the case.*

The marginal cost statement for a business making three products would look like this:

	Product	**A**	**B**	**C**
	Sales Revenue	xx	xxx	xxxx
less	Variable Costs	xx	xx	xxx
	Contribution	xx	xx	xx
less	Fixed Costs	xx	x	xx
	Profit	x	x	xx

This layout gives marginal costing some powerful advantages which are spelled out in detail below:

Advantages

- Relationship between costs, prices and sales volume is more reliably shown on a marginal cost statement than a profit and loss account.
- Businesses with a range of products can determine the contribution for each product in the range. This helps determine product profitability.
- Marginal cost statements help businesses decide whether to make the goods themselves, or buy in from other manufacturers.
- Marginal cost statements help decide where the greatest overall profit is being made.

Disadvantages

- Wrongly used; by those who don't understand the limitations, it could cause under-recovery of fixed costs and low profitability.

Here is an example of a marginal cost statement for a business with more than one service.

Example 9 Dealing with a Lossmaker

A bus company operates three limited-stop services from their depot. Management are concerned that the latest four-weekly figures continue a trend showing route X102 as unprofitable.

(i) Should you discontinue route X102?
(ii) Would the overall business be more, or less, profitable without route X102?

	Route	X101	X102	X103	Total
		£	£	£	£
	Fare Income	10000	4000	9000	23000
less	Variable Costs*	7000	2400	7200	16600
	Contribution	3000	1600	1800	6400
less	Other Costs*	1700	2200	1350	5250
	Profit (Loss)	1300	(600)	450	1150

Solution

The figures show that route X102 contributes £1,600 towards fixed costs. If service X102 were discontinued then £1,600 of contribution would be lost without any reduction in fixed costs. This would give the following position:

	£
Contribution from X101	3000
Contribution from X103	1800
	4800
Fixed Costs	5250
Loss after discontinuing X102	(450)

This means that discontinuing a lossmaker (provided it makes a positive contribution) can *worsen* the level of losses overall!

If this was a real life situation, we should check whether route X102 *really is* a lossmaker. All things being equal, route X102 appears to be carrying an unfair proportion of the fixed costs. Only further investigation would reveal whether this was fair or not.

***Note**: Variable costs comprise items like fuel, tyres and mileage related servicing costs. Other costs cover the remaining cost items which are predominantly fixed.

Of course, the example opposite does not take into account many other factors which might be involved in real life (like contractual commitments to providing the service). Nevertheless, it does indicate another useful facet of contribution theory.

Exercise 5 Dropping a Product

A company produces three products for which the following figures are available:

	Product X	Product Y	Product Z	Total
	£	£	£	£
Sales	32000	50000	45000	127000
Total Costs	36000	38000	34000	108000
Profit/Loss	(4000)	12000	11000	19000

The total cost for each product comprises 2/3 variable and 1/3 fixed cost.

The directors consider that, because product X shows a loss, it should be discontinued.

Based on the data:

(i) Should product X be dropped?
(ii) What other factors should be considered?

Compare your answer with the model on pages 149 and 150.

Chapter 7

Absorption Costing

Absorption costing is a good way of understanding how costs, volumes and prices interact. The easiest way to explain absorption costing is to use an example.

Example 10

Trevor makes wrought iron gates. Each gate costs £100 in variable costs (ie sub contract labour, material and expense). Trevor's fixed costs are £50,000 per annum. What price should Trevor charge for his gates?

Solution

To begin, we need to work out Trevor's product cost for a range of production levels. We will assume that his maximum production is 500 gates a year.

No Gates Made	Variable Cost of Gates @ £100 each	Fixed Cost	Total Cost	Cost per Gate
	£	£	£	£
1	100	50000	50100	50100
10	1000	50000	51000	5100
100	10000	50000	60000	600
150	15000	50000	65000	433
200	20000	50000	70000	350

No Gates Made	Variable Cost of Gates @ £100 each	Fixed Cost	Total Cost	Cost per Gate
	£	£	£	£
250	25000	50000	75000	300
300	30000	50000	80000	267
350	35000	50000	85000	243
400	40000	50000	90000	225
450	45000	50000	95000	211
500	50000	50000	100000	200

We can plot the cost per gate on a graph using the cost per gate on the left axis and the number of gates sold on the baseline as follows.

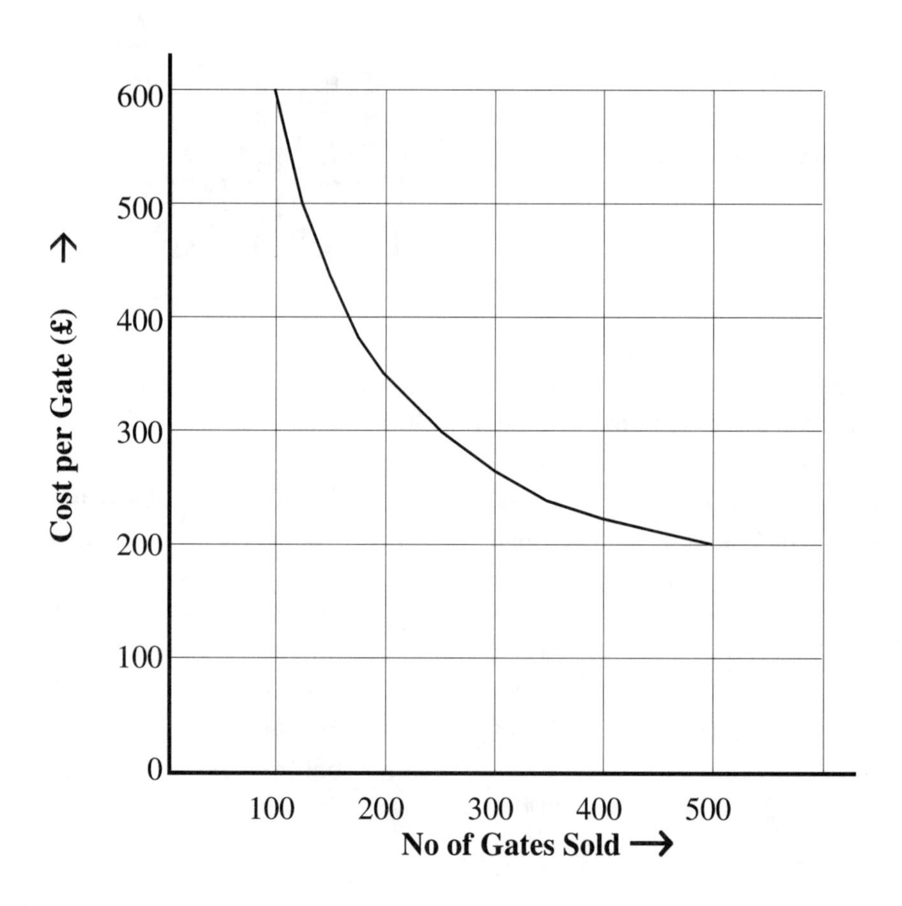

We can now add an extra axis on the right hand side labelled 'price per gate' as shown below. Note that the scale on the right hand side is the same as the scale on the left.

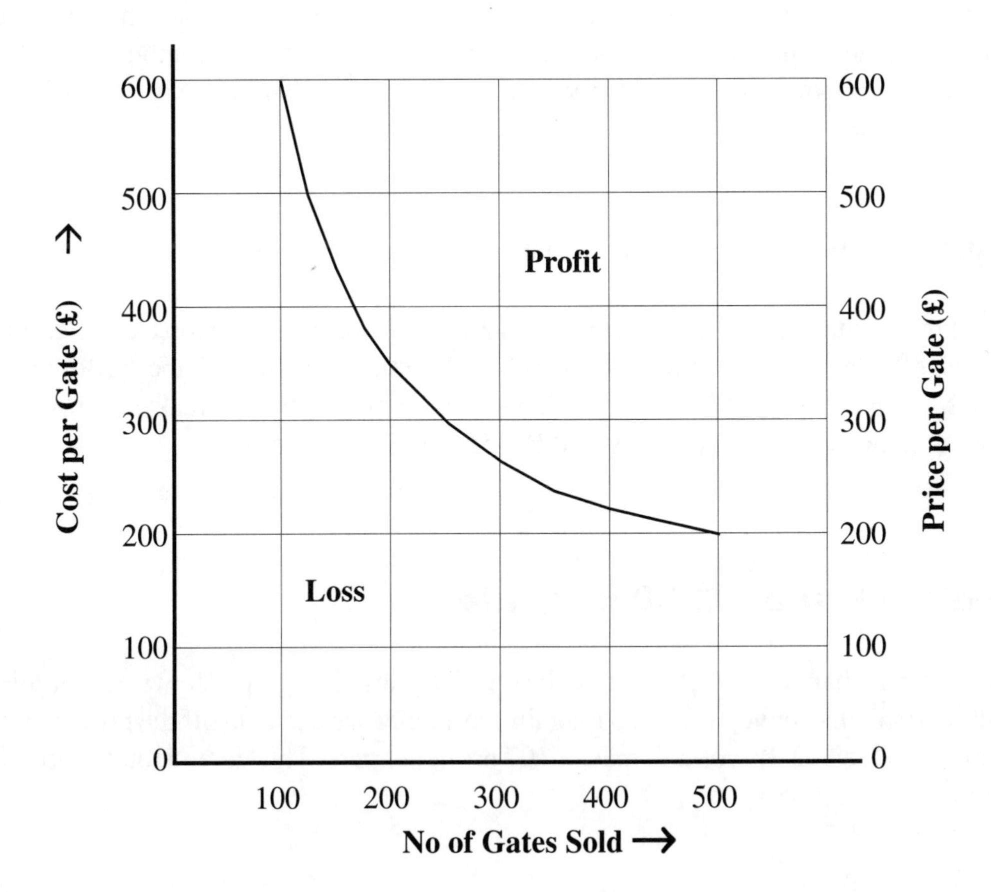

The graph now turns into a very valuable pricing tool. We can read off any combination of price (on the right hand axis) and quantity (on the bottom axis). This will tell us:

- whether the price/quantity combination yields a profit or a loss and
- how much that profit or loss is.

Trevor has decided that he could charge several prices. These are:

Very High Price £600 per gate

Trevor thinks that there may be a market for around 50 gates if he sets his price at £600. From the graph on page 50, he can tell that this price/volume combination falls below the graph line. Any order below the line makes a loss. This price is not feasible.

High Price £450 per gate

Trevor thinks that, at £450 price, he will sell around 250 gates. If we look at our graph on page 50, we can see that this option falls above the line which is the 'profitable' zone. Moreover, reading from the graph, we can see that each gate makes a profit of (around) £150 so the total profit would be 250 x £150 = £37,500.

Medium Price £350 per gate

Trevor thinks that, at £350 price, he will sell 350 gates. The graph shows us that this combination falls above the line so is again profitable. We can read off the profit from the graph to see that Trevor will make £107 profit per gate. This gives a total profit of 350 x £107 = £37,450.

Low Price £150 per gate

Trevor thinks that, at £150 price, he will sell 450 gates. If we look up this combination on the graph, we can see that this falls below the line which means that it will generate a loss. He would not find it viable to sell at £150 per gate.

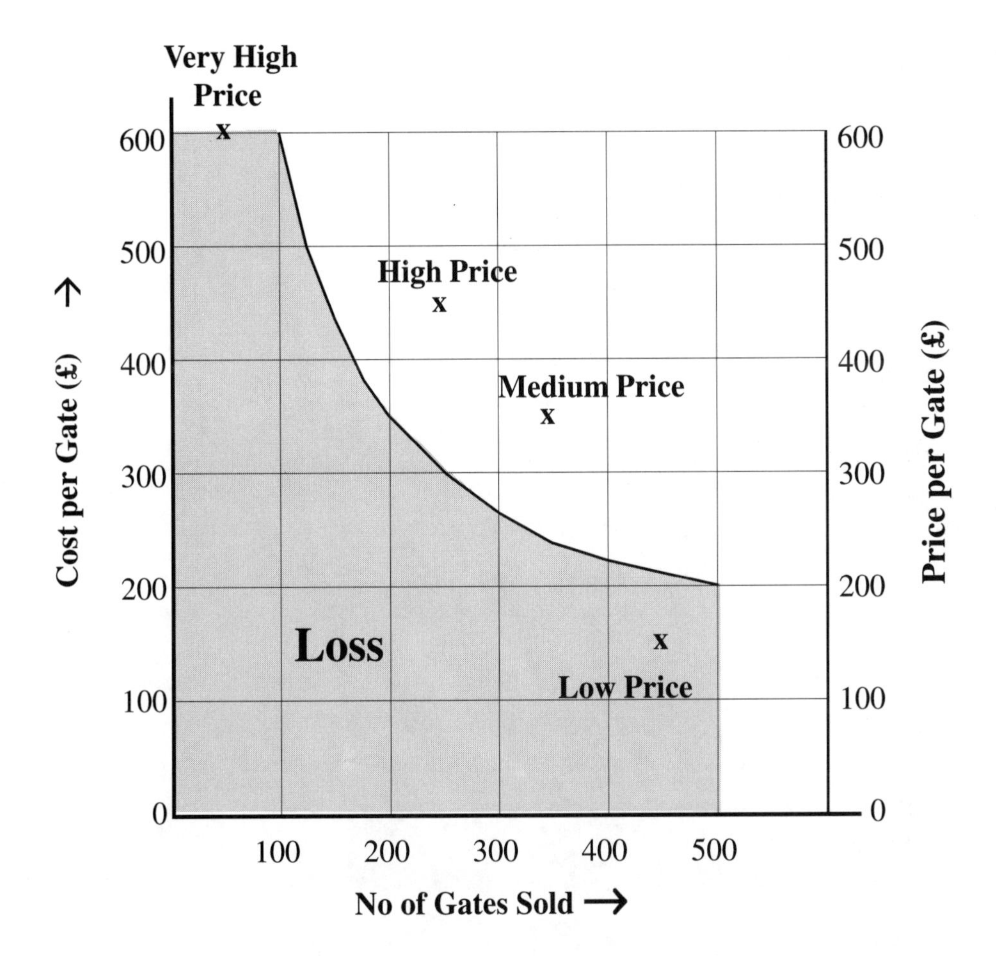

Conclusion

Based on Trevor's estimation of price and demand, he can sell anywhere between £450 and £350 per gate. He could decide to do further work on prices around this level to fine tune his final selling price.

Naturally, all estimates of sales and prices are guesswork. However, total absorption costing offers a logical framework within which you can make informed pricing decisions.

Conclusion

Chapter 8

How to Get Paid Promptly

Most firms have to provide their customers with trade credit. The aim of this part of the book is to ensure that customers do not take advantage of your willingness to provide trade credit to them.

We will look at:

- the problems caused by providing credit, including the consequences of bad debt and late payments
- how to assess whether your customers are credit worthy
- how credit control routines prevent customers from keeping your money for longer than necessary
- how to collect debt from non-paying customers through the courts
- where debt collection fails, we will see how to claim income tax and VAT relief on the bad debt.

This part of the book won't make you an instant expert at credit control and debt recovery. However, it will give you some useful guidelines to collecting debt efficiently. Good cash flow is essential for business success. We hope that these chapters will make the cash flow for you!

We will base our examples and exercises on an imaginary business called Toobie Fore. Toobie Fore is a builders' merchant specialising in timber sales. It is run by Ron Toobie and Jim Fore. Ron and Jim have been giving their customers too much credit in the past. They need to tighten up their procedures. We will see how they do it.

A Note on Terminology

Throughout this workbook we will use the terms 'debtor' and 'creditor'. People often get these two terms confused so let's get it straight from the start.

- A 'debtor' is someone who owes you money. They are in debt to you.
- A 'creditor' is someone you owe money to. They are providing credit to you.

Cracking the Credit Problem

Competitive pressures mean that many businesses have to give their customers trade credit. Credit is an unsecured, interest-free loan to customers. Uncontrolled credit is like giving customers the key to your bank account. If you have a bank overdraft on which you are being charged 15% interest, every £1,000 advanced to customers costs you around £12.50 per month in interest charges. Even if you don't have an overdraft, you are still losing the opportunity to earn interest on money 'lent' to your customers.

Cutting Down on Credit

Before we look in detail at methods of controlling credit, let's think if there are any ways in which we can cut down on the amount of credit given. For example:

- Do you really have to give credit? Is there any way that you can get customers to give you cash with their order? Can you promote a cash based business (like 'cash and carry' or factory sales outlets)?

- Could you issue an invoice but only release the goods when paid? This is called 'pro-forma' invoicing. This way your customers give you cash 'up front'.

- Can you get a deposit with the order? This way you can cut down the amount of credit given to each customer.

- Can you ask for stage payments? This will lessen the amounts outstanding (but it only works for contractors – like builders).

- Should you give credit on *every* order? It is very expensive to administer credit, especially for those customers who normally spend small amounts of money with you. You could end up spending more money on debt collection than the profit generated on small orders. Is there a certain order size below which you should insist on cash with order?

Of course you may find that, in your line of business, none of these options are available. You simply have to give credit. This is unfortunate because giving credit involves a great deal of administration. You probably know, from bitter experience, that you have to take the following steps to collect cash from your credit sale.

- raise an invoice and delivery note
- record the customer's debt in your books
- send credit notes (for returned goods) when required
- keep a list of bad payers (called an Aged Debtors report)
- send statements (which are reminders to pay the invoice)
- send chase letters to slow paying customers
- telephone debtors asking them to pay you
- record receipts from customers in your books. Pay the receipts into your bank account.

If you raise *a lot* of credit invoices, you should seriously consider a computerised accounting system. This will save a great deal of time which would otherwise be lost on credit administration. Computerised sales administration is covered in the 'Accounting With Computers' workbook in this series.

Why We Need Credit Control

The normal credit period offered to customers is 30 days. In fact, the average debt collection time is nearer 81 days because of slow payers. This extra credit period can put pressure on your cashflow.

Small firms often suffer because they have fewer administrative staff available to chase debt. They are also reluctant to apply pressure to their larger customers for fear of losing their business. Let's have a look at some of the ways in which unregulated credit can damage your business.

Bad Debts

A debt becomes 'bad' when all reasonable means of collecting that debt are thwarted. Not only do you lose the value of the bad debt, you also lose the administrative costs incurred in chasing the debt.

Few businesses appreciate the true cost of bad debt. To recover a bad debt, the business must make additional sales. The following table works this out for you.

Additional Sales Required to Recover Bad Debts

Amount of Bad Debt	Business Profitability (%)			
	5%	10%	15%	20%
	£	£	£	£
£100	2000	1000	667	500
£250	5000	2500	1667	1250
£500	10000	5000	3333	2500
£750	15000	7500	5000	3750
£1000	20000	10000	6667	5000
£1500	30000	15000	10000	7500
£2000	40000	20000	13333	10000
£3000	60000	30000	20000	15000
£4000	80000	40000	26667	20000
£5000	100000	50000	33333	25000
£10000	200000	100000	66667	50000

The left hand column lists the amount of bad debt suffered. In this example, we show bad debts ranging between £100 and £10,000. We then show four columns labelled 5%, 10%, 15% and 20%. These figures represent the profit generated by the business. For example, a business with £100,000 sales turnover showing a profit of £10,000 would have a profit of 10%. Figures for this business would all appear under the column labelled 10%.

Bad debt is cash down the drain!

The amounts shown in the body of the table reflect the extra sales which have to be made to recover the bad debt.

For example, the table shows that if your business traded at 5% profit and you incurred a bad debt of £10,000, you would have to find an additional £200,000 worth of sales just to recover your bad debt.

We can see, therefore, that one bad debt can involve you in an awful lot of work generating extra sales. Later in the book, we look at ways of avoiding bad debt in more detail.

Example 11

Toobie Fore sold a piece of timber to G Rafter and Sons. Toobie Fore purchased the timber for £95 and sold it for £100. However, G Rafter and Sons did not pay their invoice. Despite efforts to recover the debt, Toobie Fore had to write the invoice off as a bad debt. It is, therefore, obvious that Toobie Fore have lost £100 of sales. To make good this loss of material and profit, Toobie Fore need to sell twenty times the amount of that timber. This is because the profit per piece is only £5. You can confirm this by looking at the table on page 65. Look up the bad debt of £100 and check against the 5% column. You will see that the additional sales required to cover that bad debt amount to £2,000. Obviously, the smaller the profit margin, the greater the sales required to cover the bad debt.

Have a go at the following four examples. Assume that the whole of the sale price is lost as a bad debt. In this instance you need to work out the profit percentage for each case yourself. Here is the formula:

$$\text{Profit \%} = \frac{\text{Profit}}{\text{Sales}} \times 100$$

Exercise 6

Use the table on page 5 to work out how much extra sales of the same product the business needs to make to cover the lost sale.

Sale Price of Goods £	Cost of Goods £	Lost Profit %	Additional sales required to cover bad debt £
500	475		
1000	900		
3000	2550		
5000	4000		

Check your answer against the model answer on page 151.

Cost of Borrowing

It is important to keep a tight control of your cash, otherwise you could end up borrowing money to subsidise your customer's business. In fact, if your customer keeps you waiting long enough for payment, you could end up losing the whole of your profit in interest charges on outstanding debt!

The table below shows the number of days a debt needs to be outstanding to erode all profit on a sale. Here's how you use the table.

- look up the interest rate you are paying along the top of the table (eg 16%)
- look up your net profit margin on that sale down the left hand edge (eg 5%)
- look where these points intersect, eg 114 days.

This means that, if a customer keeps you waiting 114 days for payment, then your profit has been completely eroded by interest charges.

Number of days to erode all profit on a sale:

	Cost of Bank Borrowing					
Profit Margin	10%	12%	14%	16%	18%	20%
	Days	Days	Days	Days	Days	Days
2%	72	60	51	45	39	36
5%	180	150	129	114	99	90
10%	360	300	258	225	201	180
15%	540	450	387	339	300	270
20%	720	600	513	450	399	360

This table does not allow for any administrative overheads involved in chasing the debt. Allowance for this would mean that profits were eroded even more quickly.

Businesses which have been operating for a number of years tend to build up 'reserves' out of profits. Reserves are sums of money reinvested back into the business. Some of this money is used to fund debtors. Money used to fund debtors is, in effect, a transfer of reserves from your business to someone else's. Every pound that you can keep in your own account earns interest for you. If you have an overdraft then every penny kept out of your debtors' hands reduces your overdraft and saves interest payments. With overdraft rates running between 3% and 10% over bank rate, this is a handy saving for any business.

Sales Discounts

Some businesses try to minimise their outstanding debt by offering their customers a discount for prompt payment. Let's have a look at how effective this is likely to be.

Example 12

In your business would you offer a customer a discount of 2% as an inducement to pay in seven days instead of thirty days?

Yes ☐ No ☐

What effect would the discount have on your profitability?

Better ☐ Worse ☐ Much Worse ☐

You can use the following formula to work out the answer. The formula converts the discount into an annual interest rate like an overdraft or loan interest rate.

$$\mathbf{I = R \times \frac{365}{D}}$$

where:

I is the annual interest rate
R is the discount offered
D is the number of days paid early.

Let's assume that our payment terms are 30 days, but we are prepared to offer a 2% discount for cash paid within 7 days. The effective annual interest rate would be:

$$R \times \frac{365}{D} = 2 \times \frac{365}{23} = 32\%$$

We can now compare the annual interest rate we are offering our customers with the rate we can borrow from the bank. If we could borrow money from the bank at 12%, this means we are paying 20% more than we need to secure the discount. This makes the discount unattractive to us. We are better off waiting for the normal credit period of 30 days.

Discounts can affect your profits

If we were to offer the customer the same rate of interest as we could effectively borrow from the bank, ie 12%, we would only give 0.7% discount for payment 23 days early. This is unlikely to impress most customers so they probably won't pay earlier. There is a more exact method of calculating the true interest rate called the Annual Percentage Rate or APR. This would provide an even higher rate of interest than calculated using the 'simple' method above. However, APR can be difficult to calculate and the 'simple' method outlined above gives us just as clear an indication of the cost of offering a discount.

Have a go at the following question.

Exercise 7

Toobie Fore are considering offering a discount for early settlement of invoices. The normal payment terms are 60 days. A discount of 5% is offered for payment within five days. Toobie Fore have borrowings on which they pay interest of 12%. Should they offer the discount?

Work out the annual interest rate on the discount (using the interest formula). Compare your answer with the model on page 151.

$$I = R \times \frac{365}{D}$$

Should they offer the discount Yes ☐ No ☐

There can be other problems connected with offering discounts. Sometimes, customers take the discount but still pay after the normal number of credit days. You can then be left in the awkward position of trying to reclaim the discount from the customer after the event. This causes unwelcome friction and generates extra paperwork. On the other hand, if you let the customer get away with it, he will do this repeatedly which depresses your own profitability.

One way round this problem is the 'retrospective discount'. Under this system, you agree a discount with your customer but the customer has to pay the invoice in full. Provided the customer pays the invoice early enough to qualify for the discount, you rebate the amount of the discount. This eliminates arguments since the discount is only paid to the customer if he complies with the discounted payment period. This puts control into your hands. It can also offer you a slight cash flow benefit in so far as the full amount is paid into your bank but the discount is paid out somewhile later.

Perils of Overtrading

Giving too much credit could stretch our cash flow to breaking point. We hope that giving credit to customers provides an incentive for them to trade with us. However, if customers delay payment for long enough, we could have trouble in paying our own creditors – these are people we owe money to. In an extreme case, a profitable business, with full order books, could be brought down by short term payment problems. This is called 'overtrading'. The cash 'squeeze' is particularly noticeable in times of expansion. The only way round this problem in the short term is to borrow money from the bank. The long term solution is to control credit properly.

Inflation

At the time of writing this book, inflation in Britain is low. However, inflation has been as high as 27% per annum in the past. If customers pay late, they are effectively paying you in 'devalued' money. This represents a small but persistent leak in the value of money returned to you.

Risky Customers

Some businesses fail because of the 'knock-on' effects of the failure of a major customer. It can be dangerous to extend large amounts of credit to a single customer unless you are sure that customer is credit worthy. If your business relies on a few key customers, be careful to check their financial viability before advancing significant credit. This is covered in more detail in Section 3. Where possible, deal with a number of customers so that the lack of payment from one customer will not bring your business down.

Even if you have a large number of customers, you still need to avoid customers who won't pay. There are always a few unscrupulous business people who order goods or services for which they either can't or won't pay. Sometimes, they project a high profile image but actually have no asset backing. Make sure that your credit control procedures pick up these bad debt risks as early as possible. The suggestions contained within this book should help you to minimise your exposure.

Summary

We have seen that giving credit can expose us to risks in:

- bad debt
- interest charges on loans or overdraft
- the risk of overtrading.

The way to solve these problems is to:

- only extend money to customers who are able to pay
- establish good credit control routines
- recover debt from bad payers through the courts.

These topics are covered in the following chapters.

Chapter 9

Is My Customer Credit Worthy?

Only extend credit to customers who are likely to pay. Let us look at some ways of checking your customers' credit worthiness. We generally start by asking them to complete a credit application form.

The Credit Application Form

Ask your customer to complete a credit application form along the lines shown on page 76. This will serve several purposes.

- It will supply some basic information about the business. For example, limited companies are required to disclose the address of their registered office (this may be different from the trading address). Other businesses are required to disclose the name of the proprietor or senior partner and their home address. This may be needed to obtain personal credit references.

- The credit application form will give you sufficient information to approach a credit reference agency for an opinion should you wish to do so.

Forest House
Wood Lane
ELMTREE
Hants P099 9AX

CREDIT ACCOUNT APPLICATION FORM

Customers Full Name:

Trading Address:

Invoice Address (If different)

State whether *Limited Company, Partnership or Sole Trader:*

Number of employees:

Main Activity:

Maximum credit required at any one time:

Present suppliers of competitive lines:

Name and address of two trade references (not associated companies or persons connected in any manner):

Reference 1:
Reference 2:

Name and address of bankers. Account and sort code numbers:

TO BE COMPLETED BY LIMITED COMPANIES ONLY:
Registered Office Address:

Company Registration Number:
When was the company formed?
Name of directors:

TO BE COMPLETED BY ALL OTHER APPLICANTS:
Full name of proprietor/senior partner:
Home Address:

How long has the business traded?
I/We apply for a credit account with *(your business name)* subject to the payment terms and other conditions set out overleaf.

......................................Signed (Authorised Signatory)

- Ask your customer to supply two trade references. You can contact these businesses to check whether they have had difficulties with payment. Watch out, however, as they are unlikely to supply names that will give a bad reference!

- It will help you to establish a maximum credit limit to which they must adhere.

- It supplies details of their bank account. The bank can often give valuable credit information to you.

If the amount of credit requested by the customer is small and there is no reason to doubt his credit worthiness, you may decide that it is not worth taking up the bank or credit references. Only you can decide. You will still need to monitor your new customer's payment record. Don't forget that small credit limits can creep up to become big ones in time!

By the way, do you also need to establish a credit limit for *existing* customers? Is there a level of credit at which all customers (both old and new) should be subject to some form of ongoing credit checks?

People who ask for significant amounts of credit will need to be checked out further. This is done by making additional enquiries based on the credit application. Let's look at some of them in more detail.

Trade References

Your customer will have provided you with the name of two trade references. Hopefully, these are fairly representative suppliers and not a carefully cultivated set of people who receive special treatment so that they always give a good reference.

You will need to draw up a questionnaire along the lines of that shown on page 81. The example shown is quite detailed; remember, however, that the referee is under no legal or moral obligation to furnish you with the information that you require. If you ask for too much, they may simply refuse on the grounds that it is too much effort for them to complete. It's a good idea to include a pre-paid self addressed envelope. You may also mention you would be pleased to reciprocate if they wish to send a trade reference to you at any time.

Company Accounts

Your application for credit will reveal whether your new customer is a sole trader, partnership or limited liability company. If the applicant is a company, you can get a copy of the latest submitted accounts from Companies House. There is a fee for this service. Don't get too excited, however, as this avenue may not be very revealing for the following reasons.

- The accounts are abbreviated. This means there may not be sufficient information for you to base your judgement upon.

- You may not have sufficient experience to interpret the accounts.

If either of these situations arise, you may find it worth paying a fee to a credit agency who will do the work for you. At the time of writing these notes, fees are around the £50 mark, although this will depend upon how much detail you require. For this sum, you would expect to receive the basic details of the company like:

- when it was formed
- who the directors are
- the issued share capital
- the address of the registered office
- a brief analysis of the company's financial status
- whether there are any court judgements against the company

- details of any borrowings
- details of charges over the company's assets by third parties.

The agency will usually ask how much credit you intend to extend to the customer. It will then provide an assessment of the risk that this involves. An example of a credit report is shown on page 157.

Sole Traders/Partnerships

Sole traders and partnerships are not required to file accounts with any statutory body. Therefore, their accounts are not available to the public. It is still possible to obtain information and an opinion as to credit worthiness from a credit agency. A sample of such a report is shown on page 162.

Bankers References

You can obtain information about your customer from his/her bank. Bankers references are also called status enquiries. A status enquiry is a request for a bank or building society's opinion as to whether a customer could meet his/her financial commitments. Until March 1994, status enquiries were conducted between banks. If you wanted a status enquiry on a customer, you approached your bank which then approached your customer's bank to get the information. Alternatively, the enquiry could be conducted through another third party like a credit reference agency. Under the old system, banks believed that replying to a status enquiry was part of the banker's role and should be accepted as such by the person holding the bank account.

However, since March 1994 the procedure has changed. Under the new procedures, a bank can only reply to a status enquiry with the written consent of the customer. Once such consent is obtained, the bank will reply directly to the enquirer instead of an intermediary party. The new system is designed to give customers control over the information that is released to third parties. Of course, a customer's failure to provide the necessary authority may be taken as suspicious. In these circumstances, you may decide not to extend credit.

The bank's reply takes the form of an opinion as to whether the customer can meet the obligation entered into. The reply does not constitute a *guarantee* that the person will meet his/her obligations.

The reply to a status enquiry often uses indecisive or noncommittal phrases. This is because the reply could place the reporting bank in a difficult position, particularly since it is reporting on one of it's own customers. The customer is entitled to request a copy of the answer to the enquiry. You may need to ask your own bank to interpret the customer's bank's reply for you. Typical phrases used in replies include:

> **'Respectable, considered good for your enquiry.'** This is obviously a sound reply and a good indication that the bank feels your customer is perfectly able to meet the obligation you are proposing.
>
> **'Respectable, but unable to speak for your figure.'** This usually means that, although the customer has a good relationship with the bank, the bank feels that the proposed transaction may stretch the business's resources. Alternatively, it may indicate that the bank does not know much about the customer involved.
>
> **'Unable to speak for your enquiry.'** This is the worst reference and indicates that the bank has little confidence that the customer will be able to meet the commitment in full.

The charge for a status enquiry through a bank is reasonable. At the time of writing, the charges made by major banks range between £7 and £10 plus VAT per enquiry. The best way to initiate an enquiry is to use a combined enquiry and consent form. An example is shown on page 82. This form lists the information required and records the customer's consent to the enquiry.

Forest House
Wood Lane
ELMTREE
Hampshire PO99 9AX

Mr J Nail
6 Inch Road
off Tack Lane
PINNER
PXl 3SL

Trade Reference

Dear Jimmy

Re: **D Molisher**

The above-mentioned has provided us with your name as a trade reference. We would be most grateful if you could provide the answers to the questions detailed below. We are enclosing a prepaid envelope for your reply.

May we thank you for your assistance in this matter. We will, of course, reciprocate at any time.

Yours sincerely

for Toobie Fore

Name & Address of Business: D Molisher
Rubble Lane
BRICKMANSWORTH

How long known: Yrs Months

What are current credit terms: 30 Days______ 60 Days______ Longer (Please specify)______

Average sales per month to D Molisher: £100 – £500_________ £501 – £1000_____________

£1001 – £1500______ £1501+ (Please specify)______

Payment History: On Time ______ 30 days late ______ 60 days late ______ Very late ______

Name of payment contact:

Any information you may consider useful:____

Tel: (01345) 000000 Fax: (01345) 000000

COMBINED BANK REFERENCE ENQUIRY AND CONSENT FORM
Private and Confidential

Bank name Branch Address Sort code no:	**ENQUIRY TO: THE MANAGER**
Name Address Post code Tel no Fax no Date Contact name	**ENQUIRY FROM:**
Name of customer Account number (for identification purposes only) Customer's address	**INFORMATION REQUESTED ON:** I/We request your opinion as to the means and standing of and his/her trustworthiness in the way of business to the extent of £
To be completed by the person who is the subject of the inquiry Subject's full name Subject's bank Full name and address of enquirer	**CONSENT** I/We consent to Bank Plc providing reference on me/us to Signed: Date:

Do I Need Credit Insurance?

You can insure against the non-payment of debts by your customers. However, the cost of such insurance can be very prohibitive. Sometimes the terms and conditions under which the insurance company will pay out are fairly narrow. In many instances, the cost of the insurance will be greater than the amount of bad debt you are potentially exposed to. This is especially true if you have large numbers of small customers where the potential for serious bad debts is often small. However, credit insurance may be valuable if your business relies upon few customers, the failure of any one of which could put your trading operation into jeopardy.

The credit insurance company will assess the risk of bad debt from your customers and set the premium accordingly. Credit insurance usually protects against your customers becoming insolvent. It does not normally cover you against customers who are simply slow in paying their bills. The credit insurance company will not cover the full amount outstanding. It will offer a spread of premiums which generally covers between 70% and 90% of the value of the debt. There is usually an overall limit on the total amount that can be paid out.

The insurance company will go through a detailed analysis of your business to ensure that your credit control procedures minimise their potential liability under the policy. Indeed, if they are not happy with the credit control measures currently being taken, they will insist upon changes being implemented before they extend any form of insurance cover. The credit insurer will not only look at your procedures, he will also look at your customers. This may involve detailed credit checks against your major customer accounts.

Small Business Organisations/Federations

There are many small business organisations/federations which offer excellent credit management services to their members. It is often worth the price of membership just to take advantage of the facilities which may be provided at preferential rates to members.

Ongoing Credit Checks

We have discussed in this chapter ways of checking a customer's credit-worthiness. Credit checks are not only for new customers. It is important to monitor the credit-worthiness of established customers, especially if you rely on a few large orders. Don't become complacent because they have been good payers in the past, times change! Adopt the '80/20 rule'. Calculate the total value of your orders from your customers, say over the last year. Identify your largest accounts and list them in descending order of sales until you reach 80% of the total order value. These are your most important customers. Give these customers a full credit check from time to time by using the services of a credit agency. This way, you check customers by value of order and not alphabetically as this can waste time.

Chapter 10

Credit Control Routines

If your business extends credit to customers, you need a credit control routine to keep the cash flowing in. Many businesses resent the time spent on administration. However, one estimate blames 70% of all unpaid debt on firms with poor credit control systems. Many of these are small firms who can least afford bad debt and slow payment.

Effective credit control can be achieved simply by implementing a few simple procedures. However, the secret of success lies in the persistence with which they are applied. Here are the steps of credit control.

Check that the Customer is Credit Worthy

We saw in the last section that we can check whether a customer is credit worthy. It makes no sense to extend credit to a customer who is unable or unwilling to pay. The first step in a credit control routine, therefore, is to do the homework on all new customers. We need to check out the credit application, trade and bank references etc. If the customer isn't credit worthy, we will only deal with him on a cash-with-order basis. Remember that for very small accounts the above checks may not be economical.

Establish Terms and Conditions of Sale

The terms and conditions of sale set out the ground rules under which you are prepared to deal with your customers. This document is very important. If your customer fails to pay, you may commence legal action on the grounds that he is in breach of the agreed terms and conditions of sale. Because 'Terms and Conditions' is such an important document, you may decide to consult a solicitor who will draft conditions suitable for your type of business.

Terms and Conditions of Sale can include a variety of clauses (see example on page 87). However, don't simply copy down the clauses shown in our example since it may not be appropriate for your business. Typical terms include:

- The Romalpa or 'Retention of Title' clause. This states that the goods remain yours until the customer pays for them in full.

- You should include a clause setting out payment terms. This might include the right to charge interest on overdue accounts. The interest charge is usually quoted as a percentage above one of the major bank's base rates.

- Your terms and conditions will normally specify the point at which responsibility for damage to goods passes to the customer.

- You can include any number of other clauses including periods within which complaints must be notified to the supplier. You may also include situations where goods remain undelivered for reasons outside your control. The list of possible clauses is endless.

The Terms and Conditions of Sale must be agreed *prior* to entering into a transaction with your customer. Many businesses print the terms and conditions on the back of their invoices. This can cause problems in the event of a legal dispute. The customer may legitimately claim that he/she was unaware of the terms and conditions of sale when the goods were *ordered*. It is more sensible to quote the terms and conditions of sale on the back of the order form, or quotation. To avoid any charge of hiding the Terms and Conditions of Sale in 'small print', insert a box on the front of the order form with a note stating that the customer agrees to the Terms and Conditions of Sale as stated over. Request that the client signs this. Alternatively, the terms and conditions can be set out on the credit application form, if appropriate. This way your customer cannot claim that he was unaware of the Terms and Conditions of Sale under which goods or services were provided to him.

TERMS AND CONDITIONS

1 **General and Definitions**

1.1 These terms are the only terms on which Toobie Fore by whom this form is used (called 'the company') contracts with the Customer (as named overleaf).

1.2 'Goods' means all goods, parts or other things to be sold by the Company to the Customer.

1.3 The Customer will be deemed to have accepted these Terms of Business if he or his insurance company give instructions by any means for work to be done or goods to be supplied.

2 **Payment**

2.1 All goods shall be paid for upon delivery unless credit has been agreed in advance.

2.2 Interest at the rate of 2% per month (apportionable by the day) above X Bank's specified base rate will accrue on all overdue payments

3 **Retention of Title and Risk**

3.1 Goods are at the risk of the Customer as soon as they are delivered by the Company to the Customer.

3.2 Goods shall remain the sole and absolute property of the Company as legal and equitable owner until such time as the Customer shall have paid to the Company the full price thereof together with the full price of any other goods the subject of any other contract with the company and together with all storage charges and interest that may be due to the Company under this Contract or any other, and until payment in full as aforesaid has been made the Customer acknowledges that he is in possession of the goods solely as bailee for the Company.

3.3 Until the Customer becomes owner of the goods he will store them separately from his own goods or those of any other person and in a manner which makes them readily identifiable as the goods of the Company.

3.4 The Customer's right to possession shall cease if he, not being a company, commits an available act of bankruptcy or if he, being a company, does anything or fails to do anything which would entitle a receiver to take possession of any assets or which would entitle any person to present a petition for winding-up. The Company may for the purpose of recovery of the goods enter upon any premises where they are stored or where they are reasonably thought to be stored and may repossess the same.

4 **Delivery**

4.1 In these terms and conditions 'delivery' shall, unless otherwise agreed in writing, mean delivery of Goods to the business address of a Customer, the Customer's agent as stated on the Invoice, or to a carrier designated by the Customer.

4.2 Unless otherwise indicated on the Invoice or agreed in writing between the Company and the Customer.

(a) delivery in the UK or Eire will be subject to despatch charge.

(b) carriage to an address not in the UK or Eire shall be at the cost and risk of the customer.

4.3 Risk in the Goods shall unless otherwise agreed in writing pass to the customer upon delivery.

5 **Loss Or Damage**

5.1 The Company is only responsible for loss of or damage caused by the negligence of the Company or its employees.

6 **Returned Goods**

6.1 Goods will be accepted back for credit provided

(a) The Customer returns the goods within 5 working days of delivery, and

(b) The original invoice is produced, and

(c) The Customer pays the Company's current handling charges for returned goods, and

(d) The goods were not specifically ordered by the Customer.

6.2 Save as aforesaid goods will not be accepted back by the Company.

NOTHING CONTAINED HEREIN SHALL AFFECT THE STATUTORY RIGHTS OF A CONSUMER

Invoices

It is important that your invoices are designed correctly so that customers cannot use a poorly drafted invoice as a reason for non payment. A sample of a correctly drafted invoice is shown on page 89.

This is what an invoice must show:

- The invoice states clearly the name and address of the company or business issuing the invoice.
- It should show the name of the business proprietor(s) or director(s) or, alternatively, the person to whom queries regarding the invoice should be addressed.
- The invoice should show the full telephone number of the supplier including the dialling code.
- If you are VAT registered, it should show your VAT registration number.
- The invoice should have a consecutive invoice number which is used for cross referencing your own records, and for any queries raised by your customers.
- The invoice should show to whom cheques should be made payable. If the remittance is to be paid to an address different from the main address, it should show where cheques should be sent.
- If you propose to charge interest on late payment, this should be stated on the invoice. The rate of interest and the date from which interest accrues should, of course, also be included in the terms and conditions.
- The invoice should clearly describe the goods or services being billed.
- If the invoice is for goods, it should include arrangements for delivery. If you use despatch numbers then they should show the despatch number relating to these goods.

INVOICE

Forest House
Wood Lane
ELMTREE
Hampshire P099 9AX
Tel: (01234) 567890
Fax: (01234) 567891

Proprietors: Ron Toobie & Jim Fore

Invoice No:
Date:
Customer ID:
Despatch No:

Bill To:

Your Ref	Our Ref
	VAT TAX POINT:

QTY	ITEM	UNITS	DESCRIPTION	DISC %	UNIT P	TOTAL

VAT No: XXX XXXX XX
Payment Terms: Strictly 30 days Due Date: 30 April 19XX
Interest will be charged on late payment in accordance with our terms and conditions of sale
Please make cheques payable to:
Toobie Fore Builders Merchants

SUBTOTAL	
FREIGHT	
VAT (17.5%)	
MISC (interest)	
BAL DUE	

- The invoice should show the payment terms under which the invoice was raised. For example, if your credit period is 30 days then the invoice should state 'payable strictly within 30 days'. To avoid any doubt, you could include the date on which payment is due.

- If you are VAT registered, the invoice should state the tax point for VAT purposes. The significance of the tax point is explained in detail in the 'Taxation' book in the Simple and Practical series.

- The invoice should clearly state the total amount being charged for the goods or services supplied. It should also show, separately, the rate of VAT applied and the amount of VAT being charged. It is not correct to include the VAT charge in a single figure unless you are a retail outlet and the supply is less than £100 in value.

Do everything you can to make your invoice comprehensive. Hopefully, it may make your customer pay more promptly. Some businesses send two copies of the invoice. One copy can be returned with the cheque and the other copy can be retained by your customer so that they have evidence of the transaction. Many firms send brightly coloured invoices bearing their firm's logo. This can be a good technique as the invoices stand out from the others in the pile and may, therefore, warrant more prompt attention.

Invoices should be issued as soon as possible after the supply of your goods or services. Don't wait until the end of the month to issue invoices. If you do, you will be losing valuable time which you should be using to get paid promptly.

Aged Debt Analysis

Inevitably, some of your customers won't pay on time. You need a method of tracking who owes you money. You also need to know how long the money has been outstanding. There is a simple technique to do this called the aged debt analysis. The aged debt analysis forms the basis for all customer chasing procedures.

An example of a manual raised aged debt listing is shown on page 92. It summarises all unpaid invoices issued to credit customers.

An aged debtor

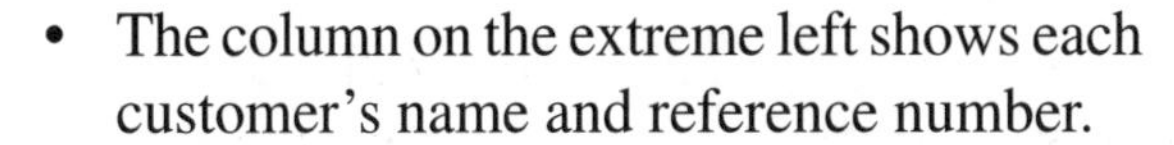

- The column on the extreme left shows each customer's name and reference number.

- The next column shows the total amount owed by that customer.

- The next column shows all invoices issued within the last 30 days. These invoices are not yet due for payment. The figure in brackets is the invoice number.

- The next four columns list all invoices which are overdue, broken down by period outstanding. The first outstanding column is overdue by up to one month. The second outstanding column is overdue by up to two months. By the time we reach the fourth 'outstanding' column (which is for invoices outstanding for over three months) we will be concerned whether we will be getting paid at all!

- You will notice that a figure in brackets appears below each amount owed. This is the invoice number. This will help you locate the invoice should it need to be referred to. It also helps you to trace one particular invoice should you have several issued to the customer at any one time.

- You may need separate aged debtor listings if you extend different periods of credit to customers. For example, some customers may be allowed 30 days credit, whilst some may have negotiated a 60 day credit period.

Toobie Fore Aged Debtor Analysis - October Credit Terms: 30 Days

Customer Name and Ref	Total Amount	Invoices Not Yet Due	Outstanding 1 Month	Outstanding 2 Months	Outstanding 3 Months	Outstanding 3 + Months	Action 1 - Statement 2 - 1st Reminder 3 - 2nd Reminder 4 - Telephone Call 5 - Warning Letter 6 - Recovery Action Implemented (State Date & Invoice No)					
							1	2	3	4	5	6
Customer 1	12000	5000 (496)	7000 (449)				4/11 (449)					
Customer 2	7000	7000 (495)										
Customer 3	6000		3000 (411)	3000 (323)			4/10 (323) 4/11 (411)	4/11 (323)				
Customer 4	10000	2000 (487)			8000 (289)		4/9 (289)	4/10 (289)	4/11 (289)			
Customer 5	14000	10000 (472)	4000 (442)				4/11 (442)					
Customer 6	1000	1000 (481)										
Customer 7	1500					1500 (204)	4/6 (204)	4/7 (204)	4/8 (204)		4/10 (204)	4/11 (204)
Customer 8	22000	12000 (392)		10000 (331)			4/10 (331)	4/11 (331)				
Customer 9	5500					5500 (234)	4/7 (234)	4/8 (234)	4/9 (234)	4/10 (234)	4/11 (234)	
Customer 10	2000	2000 (382)										
Totals	**81000**	**39000**	**14000**	**13000**	**8000**	**7000**						

- The overall totals (bottom line) provide us with an important summary of credit extended to customers. If we look at the example, we can see that total invoices issued to customers with credit accounts was £81,000. Of this total, £39,000 is within the normal credit period but a total of £42,000 is outside the normal credit term. The analysis shows us the total amount outside the credit terms, broken down by period overdue.

- Finally, the last column tells us what action has been taken to recover the debt. This is optional but very useful as you can see, at a glance, how far your credit control routine has progressed. There are six boxes, each representing different stages in your credit control routine. Each stage is recorded as it is actioned. This is a valuable management report which shows whether your credit control policy is being applied properly.

Average Number of Days Debt Outstanding

The table on page 92 gives us the information to calculate the average number of days debt outstanding. This tells you, on average, how long you are waiting for payment of your invoices. You may decide to set a target for average debt outstanding. You can then keep a check on how well you are meeting your target. Make sure that action is taken every time the average debt creeps up from the target.

Computing the average debt outstanding is very simple. First you need to estimate your annual sales. This could be taken from your cash flow projections. Alternatively, you could take the sales figure from your last set of accounts and adjust this up or down according to whether you reckon that your sales will increase or decrease in the current trading year. To calculate the average debt outstanding, simply divide debt outstanding in any one month by the total estimated sales x 365 days. If we assume total sales of £290,000, the calculation for the average debt outstanding for our example would be:

Example 13 – Calculation of average debt outstanding

Toobie Fore

Debts outstanding	£42,000
Annual sales	£290,000

Average Debt Outstanding $\frac{42000}{290000} \times 365 = 53$ days

Obviously, if Toobie Fore are extending a normal credit period of 30 days, then their customers are taking 83 days on average to pay their invoices.

Have a go at Exercises 8 and 9 following.

Exercise 8

Use the following information on transactions which took place during November to complete the aged debtor analysis on page 96. You will need to refer to the October aged debt analysis sheet (page 92) for guidance.

November Transactions

Customer 1 Paid invoice 449 £7,000. Invoice 496 £5,000 remains unpaid. Invoice 521 £5,000 issued in month.

Customer 2 Paid invoice 495 £7,000. Invoice 511 £6,000 issued in month.

Customer 3 Paid invoice 323 £3,000. Invoice 411 £3,000 remains unpaid. Invoice 502 £3,000 issued in month.

Customer 4 Invoices 289 £8,000, 487 £2,000 remain unpaid. Invoice 508 issued £4,000.

Continued

Exercise 8 (Contd)

Customer 5	Paid invoice 442 £4,000. Invoice 472 £10,000 remains unpaid. Invoice 506 £6,000 issued in month.
Customer 6	Invoice 481 £1,000 remains unpaid.
Customer 7	Invoice 204 £1,500 remains unpaid.
Customer 8	Paid invoice 331 £10,000. Invoice 392 £12,000 remains unpaid. Invoice 510 £3,000 issued in month.
Customer 9	Paid half invoice 234, balance remains unpaid.
Customer 10	Paid invoice 382 £2,000. Invoice 513 £5,000 issued in month.

Check your answer with page 152.

Exercise 9

Use the pro forma below to work out the average debt outstanding for November. Again assume total sales to be £290,000. What conclusions would you draw from the analysis for November?

Calculation Of Average Debt Outstanding For November

Debts Outstanding in November £_______

Annual Sales £_______

Average Debt Outstanding _____ x 365 =

Compare with the answer on page 153.

Toobie Fore Aged Debtor Analysis - November Credit Terms: 30 Days

Customer Name and Ref	Total Amount	Invoices Not Yet Due	Outstanding 1 Month	Outstanding 2 Months	Outstanding 3 Months	Outstanding 3 + Months	Action 1 - Statement 2 - 1st Reminder 3 - 2nd Reminder 4 - Telephone Call 5 - Warning Letter 6 - Recovery Action Implemented (State Date & Invoice No)					
							1	2	3	4	5	6
Customer 1							4/12 (496)					
Customer 2												
Customer 3							4/11 (411)	4/12 (411)				
Customer 4							4/9 (289) 7/12 (487)	4/10 (289)	4/11 (289)	4/12 (289)		
Customer 5							4/12 (472)					
Customer 6							4/12 (481)					
Customer 7							4/6 (204)	4/7 (204)	4/8 (204)	4/9 (204)	4/10 (204)	4/11 (204)
Customer 8							4/12 (392)					
Customer 9							4/7 (234)	4/8 (234)	4/9 (234)	4/10 (234)	4/11 (234)	4/12 (234)
Customer 10												
Totals												

Monthly Comparisons

It is valuable to have some indicator of how efficiently you are collecting debt. Two indicators are in common use. These are:

Debtors Turnover Ratio

This tells us how often debt is turned over in the business in a year. It is calculated as follows:

$$\text{Debtors Turnover Ratio} = \frac{\text{Sales}}{\text{Average Debtors}}$$

The higher the ratio, the better. An example is given on page 98. The debtors turnover ratio can be used to calculate the average time taken by the business to collect its total debts. This is called the average collection period (see below).

Average Collection Period

This is calculated by dividing the number of days in a year by the debtors turnover ratio.

$$\text{Average Collection Period} = \frac{365}{\text{Debtors Turnover Ratio}}$$

See the example on page 98. Your target is to get the average collection period as close as possible to the period of credit given, eg 30 days. Obviously, it will be impossible in practice to match the period of credit given. However, the average collection period provides a valuable yardstick of overall debt collection performance.

It is a good idea to monitor both ratios on a monthly basis. If you discover that the trend is getting worse, you obviously need to tighten up the debt collection routines!

In the following examples, we have only compared figures between two months to see the trend in the average collection period. In reality, we can however use all previous months figures to get a more accurate picture but you must remember to divide the debt outstanding by the total months you are considering to arrive at the average debt figure.

Example 14

Let's look at an example using the aged debtor analysis for Toobie Fore for October and November. Again, we will need to estimate the total annual sales in the business and, for this purpose, we will use our previous estimate of £290,000. We can extract the following figures from the Aged Debtor Analysis:

	1 Month	2 Months	3 Months	3 Months+	Totals
October (Previous month)	14000	13000	13500	1500	42000
November (Current month)	30000	3000	-	12250	45250

We can now work out the average debts outstanding over one month old

Average Debtors: **October** 42000
November 45250
87250 ÷ 2 = 43625

Debtors Turnover Ratio for one month $\frac{290000}{43625} = 6.64$

We can annualise the above figure to find out the average collection period
Average Collection Period $= \frac{365}{6.64} = 54.96$ Days

This means that debts over one month have an average collection period of nearly 55 days.

Have a go at Exercise 10 below.

Exercise 10

The December Aged Debtor totals for Toobie Fore are as follows:

	1 Month	**2 Months**	**3 Months**	**3 Months+**	**Total**
Dec	16000	10000	2000	2000	30000

Using the November figures as a comparative, work out:

1 The debtors turnover ratio
2 The average collection period
3 Using the November average collection period, what do the December figures tell Toobie Fore?

NB The estimated sales remain at £290,000

Check your answer with page 154.

Collection Procedures

We recommend that you use the following method to collect debt. Immediately payment is overdue, send the customer a reminder. This can be in any form; however, a duplicate copy of the invoice marked 'overdue' is a good starting point. You can buy brightly coloured stickers which are attached to the copy of the invoice, usually marked 'Account Overdue'. Alternatively, you can use a stamp to mark the invoice. A popular one carries the impression of the supplier crying large tears because the customer has forgotten to pay saying 'Please Pay Me'. At this stage, you are trying to get your invoice noticed so that it will find its way to the top of the payment file.

You can also send your customers statements. These are a summary of all outstanding invoices with the overdue ones clearly marked. You will normally raise statements once a month. However, raising statements manually is horribly time consuming. If you raise significant numbers of statements, you ought to consider installing a computerised accounting system. This will make your credit control much more efficient.

If your duplicate invoices and statements are ignored then you need to find some other way to persuade your customer to pay. You have two ways, either use a letter or a telephone call. Many people use a combination of both. Typically, you may decide to send a standard letter requesting payment timed to arrive, say, two weeks after your statement date. This should request payment within seven days. If this letter is ignored, some businesses send a further letter again requesting payment within seven days. However, you may find it more effective to telephone customers who have failed to respond to the first letter. Start the call by asking if the customer has a problem relating to the goods or service or the invoice. If there are no problems, request payment and try to agree on a payment date – preferably today! Make a note of the date of the call and record all details of the conversation – you may need these details at a later stage.

If the customer cannot pay (or perhaps cannot pay immediately), you will need to negotiate some form of settlement pattern. At this point, you could decide to withdraw credit facilities. However, care has to be exercised to make sure that a good trading relationship isn't spoiled by over enthusiastic debt enforcement. Only you can tell how far to go in light of your trading experience with that customer.

Of course some customers are experienced in delaying payment. They will use excuses like:

> *'The cheque was posted a couple of days ago'*
> *'I'm just getting around to dealing with your invoice'*
> *'Your invoice missed the computerised payment run'*
> *'The authorised signatory on the bank account is away on holiday'*
> *'We are unable to pay your invoice as we are waiting to be paid some of our outstanding invoices'.*

Don't be put off by these excuses. If the customer says that the invoice is being dealt with at that time, ask him/her politely to confirm the cheque amount and cheque number. If possible, ask them to fax you a copy of the cheque for your records.

Sometimes, the customer says the cheque has already been forwarded. If this is more than three days previously, ask them to cancel the cheque and issue a fresh one. Ask for a new cheque to be issued immediately. Also ask them to confirm the total amount and the cheque number. If the customer blames nonpayment on missing a computer run, ask if a manual cheque can be issued. If they claim a manual cheque cannot be issued, tell them that they are in breach of the agreed credit terms. Remind them that you may have to suspend their credit account until payment is received. All businesses, apart from very large institutions, are able to issue manual cheques so do not accept this excuse. Another excuse for nonpayment is that authorised signatories for cheques are unavailable or away on holiday. Request the names of those who are authorised to sign cheques and ask when they will be in the office. If this is not within a day or so, again tell them that they are in breach of their credit agreement and remind them that you may need to review their credit position.

Sometimes, a customer will tell you that you cannot be paid until their customer pays them. This indicates that the customer's cash flow is very poor. Ask them for proposals regarding payment. If possible, ask them for postdated cheques. You may wish to reconsider your credit limit for a firm which may not be able to pay you in the future!

Forest House
Wood Lane
ELMTREE
Hants PO99 9AX

31 January 19xx

Bill Toupe
20 Whig Road
Baldock
Herts

Dear Mr Toupe

Re: **Invoice No: 492**
Total Amount Outstanding: £500 + VAT (£87.50) – Total £587.50

Despite previous reminders and telephone calls, we have still not received your payment in settlement of the above invoice. You have promised payment on several occasions but no payment has been received to date.

We regret that, due to the above, we have no alternative but to consider the Small Claims Procedure in the County Court in order to recover the sum outstanding. Prior to us taking such action, we would however wish to give you one final opportunity to settle the above account. We will, therefore, delay submission of the claim to the County Court for a period of seven days from the date of this letter, in the hope that the account is settled. We will not enter into further correspondence regarding this matter other than through the County Court.

Please note that, if we are forced to take legal action, you may become liable for the costs of such action and such action, if successful, may affect your future credit rating.

Yours sincerely

for **Toobie Fore**

Tel: (01234) 567890
Fax: (01234) 567891

Have all the details to hand when talking to customers about payment. You could prepare an index card for each customer, but this involves a lot of work. Alternatively, some computer programmes provide this facility. You will need:

- the date of the original invoice
- the amount of the invoice
- the due date for payment
- a note of the dates when reminder letters were issued, or telephone calls made
- a note of any previous agreements for payment the customer has not kept to.

Record your telephone conversation and, if payment is promised, make a note in your diary so that you can check whether the amount is received as promised. This is important because if you subsequently have to take legal action, you will need to demonstrate that you have gone through all the normal collection procedures to recover the debt. Don't chase customers on the telephone unnecessarily as this could cause ill feeling. Before calling, make sure that a cheque has not been received on the morning of the day you make the telephone call. The object of telephoning is to get the customer to commit themselves to some form of timetable for payment.

If your customer does not honour the commitment given to you on the telephone, then you need to issue a final warning letter. This will provide a deadline by which the client must pay, otherwise you will consider further action. This could include Court proceedings, statutory demands, debt collection agency etc. These are dealt with in the next section. Make it clear to the customer that no further credit facilities will be extended. If they wish to continue trading with you, all future transactions will be conducted on a cash only basis. An example of a final letter is shown on page 102.

Factoring

Of course, you don't have to do all of the debt collection work yourself. You can factor your invoices – provided your sales turnover is high enough to interest the factoring company. Factoring works as follows.

You raise your invoices as normal. You then send your invoices to the factoring company who collect the debt. The factoring company will advance around 80% of the invoice value to you when they receive your invoices. They will, however, charge interest on the money advanced to you until the debt is recovered from the customer. The factoring company will also charge you a fee for their service which is generally based on a percentage of the sales turnover. Factoring is an alternative source of funding to a bank overdraft or loan.

In normal circumstances, the factoring company will not accept responsibility for bad debts. They will ask you to repay them the value of any advance which they subsequently fail to recover from the customer. However, you can extend your contract to include bad debt cover for an additional fee.

Factoring companies are useful to businesses which need to plug shortfalls in cash flow. They also offer a ready made credit control and collection service working for your business. Factoring has another advantage in that no form of security is required to cover the amounts being factored. You can, therefore, raise additional working capital from outstanding invoices without any charge by way of security being taken. The disadvantages with factoring are, obviously, the cost involved and the common perception, often misplaced, that companies resorting to factoring are in some form of financial difficulty. Customers are usually aware that factoring is in operation because the factoring company will chase them for payment of the debt rather than you yourself.

Chapter 11

Debt Recovery Through the Courts

Inevitably, a few customers will fail to pay their bills. This means that you will have to consider taking legal action against them. Before doing so, send your customer a final letter along the lines of the one shown on page 102. Some people get their solicitor to send the final letter written on the solicitor's headed paper. They believe that a solicitor's letter may carry more authority. Of course, if you use a solicitor you will have to pay the cost of sending the letter. Irrespective of who sends the final letter, you will need to take action if you do not receive payment.

Your course of action will be dictated by the size of the debt and your location.

England and Wales

If you live in England or Wales and the debt is below £3,000, you will probably want to use the small claims procedure. If the debt is over £3,000, you will need a full county court hearing.

Scotland

If you live in Scotland and your debt is below £750, you will probably want to use the small claims procedure administered by the Sheriff Court. If the debt is between £750 and £1,500, you will need to use the Summary Cause procedure which is also administered by the Sheriff Court. If the debt exceeds £1,500, you will need a full Sheriff Court hearing.

The small claims procedures in England and Wales and Scotland are broadly similar. They are both designed to provide a quick and easy way to settle disputes which have proved impossible to settle out of court. Both legal systems produce excellent guides which are available free of charge. Although the forms, claims limits and expenses differ between the two systems, the broad thrust is the same. A summary of the main differences is shown in Appendix 3 (page 171). This section focuses on debt recovery through the courts in England and Wales. For guidance on the Scottish system, read either:

- A guide to small claims in the Sheriff Courts *or*
- A guide to summary cause procedure in the Sheriff Court.

Both leaflets are available from Sheriff Courts in Scotland.

Can the Debtor Pay?

Before taking legal action, make sure that such action will result in payment of your debt. There is no point in commencing expensive legal action unless the debtor has sufficient money to meet his/her liability to you. In the event of your claim being successful, you will also seek to recover your legal costs. Although it may be very satisfying to obtain judgement against your debtor, there is little benefit to your business if you can't get any money out of him! If you are uncertain whether he has the money, you could instigate a pre-legal check on your debtor. This is a report, produced by a credit agency, which tells you whether the customer is likely to have enough money to pay you. An example is shown on pages 108 and 109. As you can see, the likelihood of success is expressed as a percentage chance of a hundred. Scores below 35% are unlikely to result in payment of your debt and percentages between 35% and 45% are borderline.

Here is one final thought before taking legal action. The threat of legal action is likely to have a terminal effect on future trading relations with your customer. Whilst you do not want to trade with someone who can't or won't pay, do make sure that the credit collection procedures listed in Chapter 10 have been exhausted. Otherwise, you could end up in an embarrassing situation when some junior or inexperienced member of staff decided to 'crack the whip' prematurely with a valued customer who had either a genuine reason for nonpayment (like a dispute over the product or service) or who hadn't paid by genuine oversight or error.

Once you have decided that you have no alternative but to take legal action and that there is a fair chance that you will get paid, you need to commence proceedings. Let's first look at how you collect debt below £3,000 using the small claims procedure.

CONFIDENTIAL STATUS REPORT

SUPPLIED BY
FCC CREDIT MANAGEMENT
(A DIVISION OF FCC MANAGEMENT SERVICES LTD
REGISTERED IN ENGLAND No1766258
FEDERATION HOUSE 1 THE BRIARS
WATERBERRY DRIVE WATERLOOVILLE
PORTSMOUTH HANTS PO7 7YH
TEL: (01705) 232113
FAX: (01705) 232126

SAMPLE EPIC PRE-ISSUE CHECK

Date: Date of Report
Our Ref: ABO513/0141/O1
Your Ref: 6609

PRE-ISSUE EPIC REPORT

DEBTOR: MR C REEVES

AMOUNT: £358.79

Further to your recent instruction regarding a pre-issue check for the above named debtor, please find listed below the results of our Electronic Pre-Issue Check.

FCC now have the facility to access 'on-line' information that will indicate the percentage probability of successful action through litigation, for a given debt amount.

This report has been compiled using one of the largest on-line electronic pre-issue check systems available in this country.

It is agreed that all information is furnished for your private use only and is supplied in confidence. The client agrees with the Agency that all such information is supplied on the express understanding that the Agency is not held responsible for damage or loss arising from insufficient or inaccurate information furnished to the Client whether by reason of mistake or negligence of the Agency or its Servants

CONSUMER CREDIT LICENCE No 339486

CONFIDENTIAL STATUS REPORT

SUPPLIED BY
FCC CREDIT MANAGEMENT
(A DIVISION OF FCC MANAGEMENT SERVICES LTD)
REGISTERED IN ENGLAND No 1766258
FEDERATION HOUSE 1 THE BRIARS
WATERBERRY DRIVE WATERLOOVILLE,
PORTSMOUTH HANTS PO7 7YH
TEL: (01705) 232113
FAX: (01705) 232126

Some of the characteristics that the percentage probability is based upon relate to:

Electoral Roll
County Court Judgements & Court Decrees
Geodemographic
Court actions throughout UK
Derive Data (Post Code info)
Credit Searches
Trace Searches
File Activity

This facility is recalculated each time the system is accessed and, therefore, provides an up to date and dynamic indication based on the current status of an individual.

Our findings are as follows:

EPIC PROBABILITY 58%

We would strongly recommend that a probability factor of less than 35% should not be pursued via litigation as the likelihood is that, although judgement may be obtained, enforcement may not be possible due to lack of assets on which to levy. The decision to instigate legal proceedings on borderline cases (35–45%) must be with the creditor.

Making a Small Claim in England and Wales

The Procedure

The small claims procedure is administered by the County Court system in England and Wales. In Scotland a similar procedure is administered by the Sheriffs Court. Both Courts issue you with all the documentation you require and produce an excellent series of leaflets which will guide you through the procedure and cover any other eventualities that may arise.

The initial claim is placed with the County Court in your area. But, if the debtor disagrees with your claim and is not resident in your area, the case could be transferred to the County Court in the debtors area. You will have to pay certain costs before the Court will process your claim. Examples of these fees are shown on pages 123 and 124.

Your claim to the Court is entered on a form called a 'County Court Default Summons' (Form N1). A copy of this form is shown on pages 113 and 114. You need to complete three copies of this form:

- one for your own records
- one for the Court
- one which will be sent to your debtor.

Scotland uses its own forms which differ according to the amount and the type of debt. The purpose of the forms however is similar.

Be sure to get the correct (full) name of the debtor and the exact address. This is because most default summonses are issued by post. If the address is not correct, the debtor may be able to delay or defend your claim by arguing that the summons was never received. If the debtor is a limited company, you must send the summons to the registered office of the company. The registered office of a limited company is often different to that of the trading address. You should be able to find this address on the company's letterhead, or an invoice. If this fails, you can get the address of the registered office from a trade directory or from the Registrar of Companies House.

If your debtor is a partnership, be sure to address your claim to all of the partners in the business, not just one particular partner. This is because, at the time of writing, all partners are 'jointly and severally liable' for debts relating to their business. If you are successful in your claim, all the partners in the business will be liable for payment of your debt. If you issue a claim against only one partner and he or she does not pay, then you will be unable to claim your debt from the other partners who may be in a position to meet the liability.

The County Court Default Summons requires you to provide details of your claim against the defendant. You need to complete a brief statement explaining why you consider the debtor owes you the amount outstanding. Also enter on the form the amount of the debt and add on your court fees so that your total claim will be the debt plus any fee which has been paid. Once matters are put onto a legal footing, the person issuing the claim will be known as the Plaintiff and the debtor will be known as the Defendant.

Once the Court has received your claim, it will issue a form (N205A) which is a receipt for your fee. They will also give you a reference number for your claim which is known as your 'Plaint No'. The Court will normally issue the summons to your debtor by post, although you can serve the summons yourself or ask the Court Bailiff to deliver the summons if you are prepared to pay an extra fee. The summons encloses a form which requires the Defendant to reply to the Court within 21 days of receiving the form. The time starts on the day after the Defendant receives the summons. The Court will notify you of the date the summons is served by forwarding to you a form known as a Notice of Service (E222). If the summons cannot be delivered and is returned by the Post Office, the Court will issue a form advising of non service. If you wish to continue your claim, you must find out the correct address for service of the summons. The Defendant must receive the summons within four months of the date you started your claim unless you ask the Court for more time.

What if No Reply is Received?

If no reply is received to the summons within the 21 day period, you can ask the Court to send an Order to the Defendant ordering payment of the debt. This Order is an instruction to the Court to enter Judgement against a Defendant by default. When you ask for Judgement to be made against the Defendant, you will need to decide on how you wish the debt to be paid. Will the Defendant be able to settle your debt in full straightaway? If you have any doubts, you can tell the Court that you are willing to accept payment by instalments. Once the court receives your instruction, it will issue a Judgement Order against the Defendant which will tell the Defendant how much to pay and where the funds are to be paid to.

What if the Defendant Admits the Claim?

If the Defendant accepts your claim, he may file an Admission with the Court on form N9A (see Appendix 2 – pages 165 and 166). This Form of Admission will be forwarded directly to you by the Defendant and not to the Court. On the Form of Admission, the Defendant may ask to pay the debt by instalments or at some future date. It is up to you to decide whether you accept the proposal set out by the Defendant. If you agree with the offer, you may ask the Court to issue an Order to pay the debt that you are owed. This is known as entering Judgement on acceptance. To assist you, the Form of Admission requires the Defendant to set out all details of his income and expenditure, and list all his assets. The Judgement Order tells the Defendant how much, where and when to pay the money. If you do not accept the Defendant's proposals, you may object to the offer stating how much you will be willing to accept and when. These proposals will then be forwarded to the Court with a copy of the Defendant's admission. The Court will look at the information provided and determine a fair way for the Defendant to pay. This is known as entering Judgement by Determination.

County Court Summons

Case Number *Always quote this*

In the

County Court

The court office is open from 10am to 4pm Monday to Friday

Telephone:

(1) Plaintiff's full name address

(2) Address for service (and) payment *(if not as above)* Ref/Tel no.

(3) Defendant's name address

Seal

This summons is only valid if sealed by the court
If it is not sealed it should be sent to the court

What the plaintiff claims from you

Brief description of type of claim

Particulars of the plaintiff's claim against you

Signed
Plaintiff('s solicitor)
(or see enclosed particulars of claim)

Amount claimed		
Court fee		
Solicitor's costs		
Total amount		
Summons issued on		

What to do about this summons

You can
- **dispute the claim**
- **make a claim against the plaintiff**
- **admit the claim in full and offer to pay**
- **pay the total amount shown above**
- **admit only part of the claim**

For information on what to do or if you need further advice, please turn over.

Keep this summons. You may need to refer to it

N1 Default summons (fixed amount) (Order 3, rule 3(2)(b))

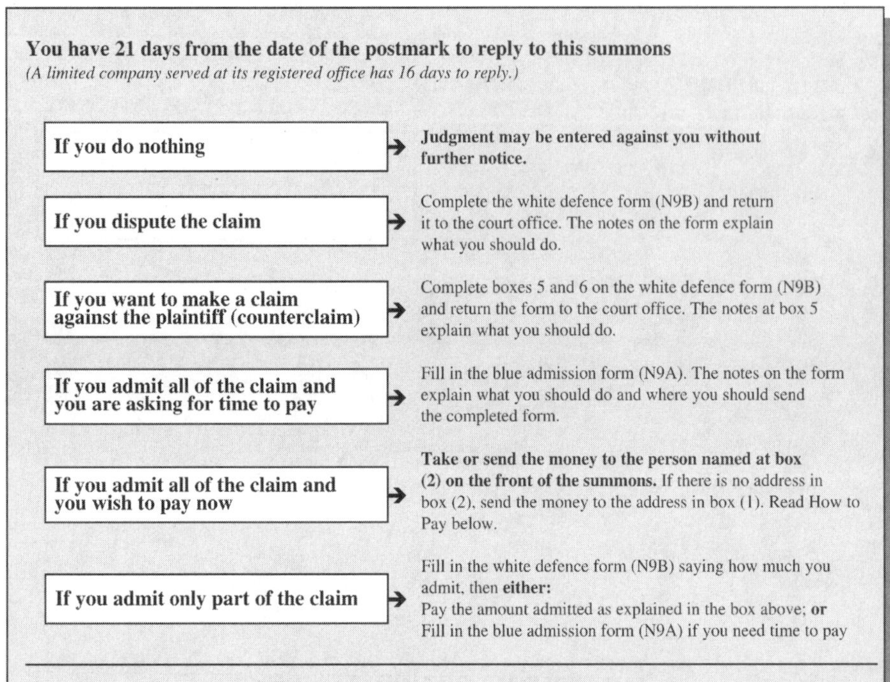

You have 21 days from the date of the postmark to reply to this summons

(A limited company served at its registered office has 16 days to reply.)

If you do nothing →	**Judgment may be entered against you without further notice.**
If you dispute the claim →	Complete the white defence form (N9B) and return it to the court office. The notes on the form explain what you should do.
If you want to make a claim against the plaintiff (counterclaim) →	Complete boxes 5 and 6 on the white defence form (N9B) and return the form to the court office. The notes at box 5 explain what you should do.
If you admit all of the claim and you are asking for time to pay →	Fill in the blue admission form (N9A). The notes on the form explain what you should do and where you should send the completed form.
If you admit all of the claim and you wish to pay now →	**Take or send the money to the person named at box (2) on the front of the summons.** If there is no address in box (2), send the money to the address in box (1). Read How to Pay below.
If you admit only part of the claim →	Fill in the white defence form (N9B) saying how much you admit, then **either:** Pay the amount admitted as explained in the box above; **or** Fill in the blue admission form (N9A) if you need time to pay

Interest on Judgments

If judgment is entered against you and is for more than £5000, the plaintiff may be entitled to interest on the total amount.

Registration of Judgments

If the summons results in a judgment against you, your name and address may be entered in the Register of County Court Judgments. **This may make it difficult for you to get credit.** A leaflet giving further information can be obtained from the court.

Further Advice

You can get help to complete the reply forms and information about court procedures at any county court office or citizens' advice bureau. The address and telephone number of your local court is listed under "Courts" in the phone book. When corresponding with the court, please address forms or letters to the Chief Clerk. Always quote the whole of the case number which appears at the top right corner on the front of this form; the court is unable to trace your case without it.

How to pay

- **PAYMENT(S) MUST BE MADE to the person named at the address for payment quoting their reference and the court case number.**
- **DO NOT bring or send payments to the court. THEY WILL NOT BE ACCEPTED.**
- You should allow **at least 4** days for your payments to reach the plaintiff or his representative.
- Make sure that you keep records and can account for all payments made. Proof may be required if there is any disagreement. It is not safe to send cash unless you use registered post.
- A leaflet giving further advice about payment can be obtained from the court.
- If you need more information you should contact the plaintiff or his representative.

To be completed on the court copy only

Served on

By posting on

Officer

Marked "gone away" on

Printed in the UK for HMSO 08/93 D 8423858 C10,000 36625

What if the Defendant Admits Only Part of the Claim?

In some cases, the Defendant may only admit part of your claim for the debt. He will complete the admission form and with it a defence form. You will receive copies of these forms, together with form N225A (see Appendix 2 – page 169) which will allow you to reply to the part admission. If you accept the part admission, the Court will make an order to pay you. This is known as entering Judgement on Acceptance. If you disagree with the part admission, you must say why you disagree and state how much you are prepared to accept and when it should be paid. The Court will then consider the information provided by the Defendant and the reasons that you were given for not accepting the offer and determine a fair way for the Defendant to pay. This is also known as entering Judgement by Determination.

What if the Defendant Enters a Defence?

The Defendant may enter a defence against your claim. In this case, he will complete a form Form N9B which is issued with the Summons (see Appendix 2 – pages 167 and 168) giving reasons why he feels that your claim is not acceptable. If you do not accept the defence, you will need to advise the Court. The case will then be handled by a District Judge. The District Judge will consider both sides of the case and decide what action should be taken. The District Judge could list the case for an Arbitration Hearing, in which case you will be notified. The notification will tell you what you need to do to prepare for the Hearing. Alternatively, the Judge could decide that a preliminary Hearing is appropriate. He will then make an appointment to see you and the Defendant to see if matters can be resolved between you. Finally, if the Judge decides that the case is too difficult to be handled under the Small Claims procedure, he may order that the trial be heard in open Court. If this decision is taken, you may decide to consult a solicitor. Most cases are settled by arbitration. All parties sit down with the District Judge on an informal basis, and settle matters between them.

Claims Over £3,000 in England and Wales

The small claims procedure is designed to avoid the necessity of a full court hearing. In England and Wales, debts over £3,000 still follow the same procedure except that a defence has to be heard in Open Court. Even if the debt does exceed £3,000, it may still be possible to go to arbitration provided both parties agree.

One very real difference, however, arises with regard to solicitors' costs. Under the small claims procedure, solicitors' costs cannot be reclaimed. However, outside of the small claims procedure, solicitors' costs can be awarded. Both Plaintiff's costs *and* Defendant's costs can be awarded against either party. Before entering litigation, therefore, you must be sure that:

- you can afford the legal costs of pursuing your claim
- you are satisfied that you will be able to recover your legal costs from the Defendant.

Remember, an invalid claim could result in you not only having to pay your own costs, but also those of the Defendant. If the debt exceeds £25,000, it is usually referred to the High Court. Legal advice in this context should definitely be sought!

In Scotland debts of between £750 and £1,500 are dealt with under the Scottish Summary Cause procedure. This is similar to the Scottish small claims procedure except that the debt has to be heard in open court. Costs can be awarded against either party. If the debt exceeds £1,500 it is still heard in the Sheriffs court but the procedure is more complicated. A solicitor is recommended for claims over £1,500.

Enforcing Judgement

Once you have obtained legal Judgement against your debtor, the Court will either order your debtor to pay the debt in full, or by some other method which you have agreed. If the debtor still fails to pay you after the court judgement, you will need to resort to some method of debt enforcement. Remember, there will be additional 'up front' costs in enforcing your Judgement through the County Court. Here are some methods of enforcement.

Warrants of Execution

A Warrant of Execution is an instruction to the Court Bailiff to visit the Defendant's home or business address to try and collect the debt which you are owed. If he cannot get the money, he can apply Distraint Action. This means that the Bailiff can take goods from the debtor to sell at a public auction in order to raise money to pay your debt. Alternatively, if the Defendant offers settlement by a certain date or gives a postdated cheque, the Bailiff may take what is termed 'walking possession' of the goods. This imposes a temporary legal charge on the goods preventing the Defendant from selling them until either payment is received or the cheque clears. If there are any problems then the Bailiff can take possession of those goods. A Bailiff will only seize goods which are owned by the debtor outright. If, for example, goods are subject to an HP agreement, these cannot be seized because the HP company may have a claim on the goods. If the Bailiff does seize goods, you will find that the value of goods seized is likely to be far in excess of the actual debt which you are owed. This is because goods sold at public auction tend to realise less than their market value. All costs will need to be recovered (including the auctioneer's) out of the proceeds. If you suspect that your debtor does not have sufficient assets to pay your debt then other forms of recovery should be examined.

Attachment of Earnings

An Attachment of Earnings award only works where your debtor is in paid employment. The Order is an instruction to the debtor's employer to deduct an amount of money from the Defendant's earnings each week (or month) and forward this directly to the Court. The Court then remits this amount to you. An Attachment of Earnings Order means that the money is deducted by the employer directly, without the debtor getting his hands on the money first. These types of Order can often cause problems for the employee. Firstly, because the employer becomes aware of the debt and, secondly, the employer has the cost of complying with the Court Order.

Garnishee Order

If you discover that the Defendant has a Bank or Building Society account with sufficient funds to settle your debt, you can apply for a Garnishee Order. This Order will take money directly from the Bank or Building Society account in order to settle your debt. As this Order is made by the Court, the debtor cannot prevent the Bank or Building Society complying with the Order. If you can satisfy the Court that you know of a third party who owes the Defendant money, then the Garnishee Order can be applied to that third party. This means that they pay your debt instead of the Defendant's debt. This often happens where your debtor is unable to pay you because he, in turn, has not been paid by someone else.

Charging Order

A Charging Order issues a charge over the assets of your debtor. He can be prevented from selling any assets. If assets are sold, the debt would then be deducted directly from any sale proceeds. Under a Charging Order, you can request that the Court orders a forced sale of assets in order to satisfy your debt. A table setting out the fees for the above orders, and for small claims generally, is set out on pages 123 and 124.

Oral Examinations

If you are not certain of your debtor's circumstances, you can ask the Court to have your debtor examined under oath to discover his or her ability to pay the debt. This is known as an Oral Examination. Failure of your debtor to attend the Oral Examination can result in their being sent to prison for being in contempt of Court.

The purpose of an Oral Examination is to find the most effective way to enforce Judgement. There is a fee to be paid for an Oral Examination. Upon receipt of this fee, the Court will issue an Order requiring the debtor to attend, bringing documents relating to his/her finances. It is better that you, the creditor, attend the Oral Examination but, if you are nervous about facing your debtor, the Registrar of the Court will conduct the examination for you and, for a further fee, provide written confirmation of your debtor's answers signed by your debtor.

The questions asked depend on whether the debtor is a limited company or an individual. If the debtor is a limited company, then one of the directors will be required to attend. In this case, questions may only seek information regarding the assets of the company and not the individual directors.

If the debtor is an individual (or partner), you may ask for information concerning both their business and their personal assets. The questions will relate to the following broad areas.

- Details of any Bank or Building Society accounts held, together with any details of other assets or investments like stocks and shares.

- Details of any property owned, together with details as to legal title and any loans secured against it.

- Details of other tangible assets held by the debtor like vehicles, furnishings, pictures, any valuable collections, TVs, videos, sound systems etc.

Remember, it may not be possible to sell assets which are the subject of a hire purchase agreement. The Defendant will be asked if there is any other legal action pending against him, or any previous Court Orders. If you are considering applying for an Attachment of Earnings Order, then you need to obtain details of the individual's employment. This should include the name and address of the employer, any pay reference number and details of their salary.

The Oral Examination can be a big help in deciding what form of enforcement action you intend to take and whether such action is likely to prove successful.

Exercise 11

Bill Toupe still has not paid his bill to Toobie Fore (see the final letter on page 102). From the following information, work out:

(i) How much Toobie Fore need to claim in court to recover both their debt and costs. (See pages 123 and 124 for costs.)

(ii) What method of enforcement should Toobie Fore choose to secure payment of their debt. A summary of costs is shown on pages 123 and 124.

Toobie Fore have issued a default summons and obtained judgement in the County Court. The debt was for £500 plus VAT, giving a total amount of £587.50. Toobie Fore have requested an oral examination which yielded the following answers.

1 How do you trade and how long have you traded?
I have been a self-employed carpenter for 10 years.

Continued

Exercise 11 (Contd)

2 What Bank and Building Society accounts do you have? What are the current balances?

I have a business account with XX Bank whose address is XX. The account number is 24956785. The current balance on this account is £2,480 overdrawn.

I also have an investment account with the XX Building Society whose branch address is XX. The account number is 1129467X. The current balance on this account is £875.

3 Do you own any property?

Yes, I have my own house.

4 When did you purchase this house?

One month ago.

5 What is the value of the property?

£65,000

6 Do you have a mortgage and, if so, how much and to whom?

Yes. £50,000 to the XX Building Society.

7 Is the house in your sole name?

Yes.

8 How much is your mortgage each month?

£325 plus an endowment policy of £85 per month.

9 Do you have any other investments, ie stocks and shares, premium bonds?

No, I sold all my shares to buy my house.

Continued overleaf

Exercise 11 (Contd)

10 Do you own any motor vehicles? If so, how much did it cost? How old is it? Is there any outstanding finance on it?
I own a pickup truck which I use in my business. It was purchased new last month under a hire purchase agreement with the XX credit company. It cost £12,000 and the outstanding credit is £10,000 as I put a deposit of £2,000 down. I will be paying £268 per month for the truck. The first payment will be made this month.

11 Do you own any furniture, TV, videos etc? If so, are any of these on HP? If so, what items, and how much is outstanding?
I purchased all my furniture for the new house on a HP agreement. The furniture cost £4,900 and I paid a deposit of £1,000. The balance is outstanding on the hire purchase agreement. The monthly payment is £190. I have a TV, video and stereo system, all of which are on hire purchase. They cost £1,800 in total and I owe £1,500 on hire purchase. The monthly repayment is £95.

12 Do you hold any other assets, ie antiques, collections etc not mentioned above?
I only have a record collection worth, say, £300.

13 Do you have any other debts not mentioned above or any other Court Orders against you?
No.

14 Are you married, single, divorced or separated?
I am single.

15 Do you have any children?
No.

Check your answer with page 155.

Examples of Court Fees

Scotland

To issue a Default Summons when a debt is owed	
• Claims under £50	Fee £5
• Claims between £50 and £750	Fee £19
• Claims between £750 and £1,500	Fee £26
• Service of summons by a Sheriff Officer (where applicable)	Fee £5.50

England and Wales

Starting Your Claim	
• To issue a default summons when the debt is not more than:	**Fee**
£100	£10
£200	£20
£300	£30
£400	£40
£500	£50
£600	£60
£1,000	£65
£5,000	£70
Unlimited	£80
• To ask the court bailiff to serve a document	£10
• Fee payable when a trial date of your case is fixed	£50
• Notice of appeal or application to set aside arbitrator's award	£20

Enforcing Judgement

	Fee
• To issue warrant of execution to recover a sum of money	
– not more than £125	£20
– more than £125	£40
• To issue warrant for recovery of land or property	£80
• To issue application for an attachment of earnings order	£50
• To issue application for a charging order	£25
• To issue application for a garnishee order	£25
• To issue a judgement summons	£25
• To issue application for an oral examination	£30

Bankruptcy and Company Winding Up

	Fee
• To issue bankruptcy petition in respect of your own affairs	£25
• To issue bankruptcy petition against someone who owes you money	£55
• To issue petition to wind up a company which owes you money	£55
• To issue application in bankruptcy/company winding up proceedings	
– heard by a District Judge	£20
– heard by a Circuit Judge	£20

Chapter 12

Statutory Demands, Insolvency and Bankruptcy

The Statutory Demand is a little known, but highly effective, means of obtaining payment for debts. You can issue a Statutory Demand if the debt exceeds £750 and you have been unsuccessful in collecting payment by the normal routes. A Statutory Demand for payment was created under Sections 123 and 222 of the Insolvency Act of 1986. An example is shown on pages 127 to 129.

The Statutory Demand is a formal warning to your debtor. It is a declaration that you believe his/her company or business is either insolvent or bankrupt. Unless the debtor responds within 21 days, you will take formal proceedings to either wind up their company or, if they are an individual, bankrupt them.

A Statutory Demand is a very cost effective means of recovering a debt. Pre-printed Demands such as those shown on pages 127 to 129 are readily available for a matter of pence. The recipient of the Demand must respond to it within the allocated time, otherwise you can petition for winding up or bankruptcy. In many instances, the debtor will not be insolvent but, even so, they must respond. The threat of insolvency can be a useful tool to extract payment from a company or individual. This applies especially to those who want to project a high profile successful trading appearance. If the debtor is genuinely unable to pay, you need to decide whether to wind up the company or bankrupt the individual. We will look at the factors affecting this decision later in this section.

It is important that the debt which you are claiming is an undisputed and identifiable fixed sum. You could not serve a statutory demand for, say, a claim for damages for loss of business as this may not be easily quantifiable.

The Statutory Demand must be served upon the debtor, just like the Judgement Summons. However, unlike the Judgement Summons, you cannot post the Statutory Demand. It must be handed directly to the debtor. If the debtor is a limited company, the Statutory Demand must be served at the registered office of the company.

The Statutory Demand will test the ability of the debtor to pay because the consequences of not paying are so drastic. Company directors and individuals will, therefore, take this document very seriously and it will, obviously, affect future trading relations. Statutory Demands should not be used lightly. Nor should they replace normal means of debt collection.

Let's move on now to see how you would wind up your debtor. Here are a couple of definitions before we start.

Individuals and partnerships are wound up by the process of *bankruptcy*. Companies are wound up in the process of *liquidation*.

How to Initiate Bankruptcy Proceedings

Bankruptcy enables you to recover debt from both the business assets and the personal assets of a sole trader or a partnership. The debt must be over £750 before you can petition for bankruptcy. A Bankruptcy Petition does not give access to assets over which a third party holds a prior charge (eg a mortgage on a house).

Rule 4.5 **Form 4.1**

Statutory Demand under section 123(1) (a) or 222(1) (a) of the Insolvency Act 1986.

Notes for Creditor

- If the creditor is entitled to the debt by way of assignment, details of the original creditor and any intermediary assignees should be given in part B on page 3.
- If the amount of debt includes interest not previously notified to the Company as included in its liability, details should be given including the grounds upon which interest is charged. The amount of interest must be shown separately.
- Any other charge accruing from time to time may be claimed. The amount or rate of the charge must be identified and the grounds on which it is claimed must be stated.
- In either case the amount claimed must be limited to that which has accrued due at the date of the demand.
- If signatory of the demand is a solicitor or other agent of the creditor the name of his/her firm should be given.
- Delete if signed by the creditor himself.

WARNING

- **This is an important document. This Demand must be dealt with within 21 days of its service upon the company or a winding-up order could be made in rest of the Company.**
- **Please read the Demand and notes carefully. There are additional notes overleaf.**

Demand
To
Address

This demand is served on you by the creditor:
Name
Address

The creditor claims that you owe the sum of £
full particulars of which are set out on page 2.

The creditor demands that the company do pay the above debt or secure or
compound for it to the Creditor's satisfaction.

Signature of individual

Name (in Block Letters)

Date

Position with or relationship to Creator:
I am authorised to make this demand on the creditor's behalf
Address

Telephone number
Reference number
N.B. The person making this demand MUST complete the whole of this page, page 2 and parts A and B (as applicable) on page 3.

Winding Up (Compulsory) 1	Page 1	

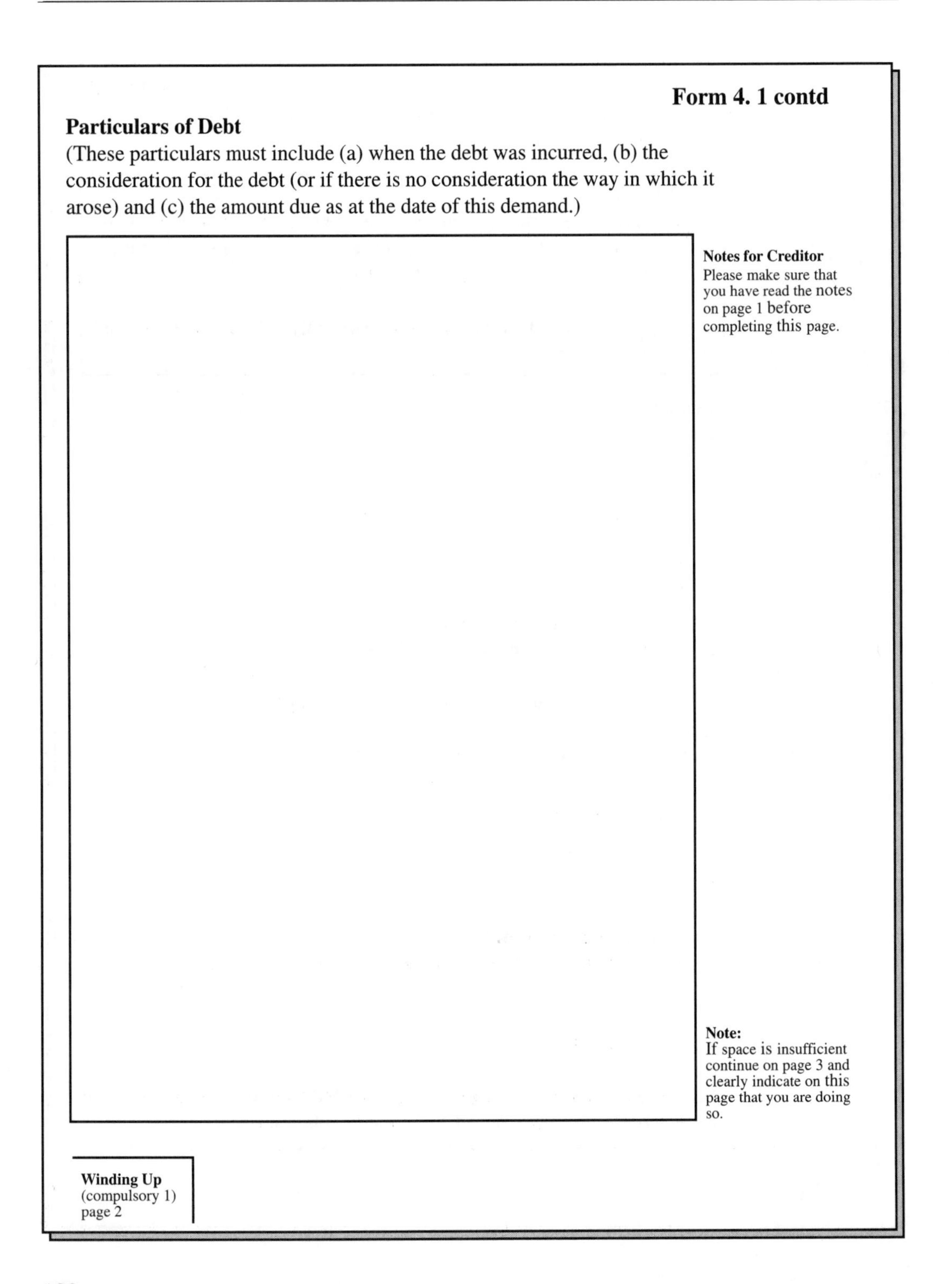

Form 4. 1 contd

Particulars of Debt

(These particulars must include (a) when the debt was incurred, (b) the consideration for the debt (or if there is no consideration the way in which it arose) and (c) the amount due as at the date of this demand.)

Notes for Creditor
Please make sure that you have read the notes on page 1 before completing this page.

Note:
If space is insufficient continue on page 3 and clearly indicate on this page that you are doing so.

Winding Up
(compulsory 1)
page 2

PART A

The individual or individuals to whom any communication regarding this demand should be addressed is/are

Name
(BLOCK LETTERS)
Address

Telephone Number
Reference

PART B

For completion if the creditor is entitled to the debt by way of assignment

	Name	Date(s) of assignment
Original Creditor		
Assignees		

How to comply with a statutory demand

If the Company wishes to avoid a winding up petition being presented, it must pay the debt shown on page 1 of this notice within the period of 21 days after its service upon the Company. Alternatively, the Company can attempt to come to a settlement with the Creditor. To do this the Company should:-

- inform the individual (or one of the individuals) named in Part A above immediately that it is willing and able to offer security for the debt to the creditor's satisfaction;

OR

- inform the individual (or one of the individuals) named in Part A immediately that it is willing and able to compound for the debt to the creditor's satisfaction.

If the Company disputes the demand in whole or in part it should:

- contact the person named in Part A immediately.

REMEMBER! THE COMPANY HAS ONLY 21 DAYS FROM THE DATE OF SERVICE ON THIS DOCUMENT BEFORE THE CREDITOR MAY PRESENT A WINDING UP PETITION.

Winding Up
(Compulsory 1)
Page 3

Before initiating bankruptcy proceedings, be sure that you stand a chance of getting your money. There may be other creditors ranking above you, the unsecured trade credit creditor, when it comes to distributing money. These preferential creditors would normally include the taxman, the bank and anyone lending money secured on property or other assets of the business. This means that their debt will be settled before yours. If uncertain, you could consult a credit agency which may be able to provide a confidential status report on your debtor. This should give a clue on the financial status of your debtor and also identify any registered charges held on their assets. This will help gauge whether your petition is likely to prove successful.

Bankruptcy

A Bankruptcy Petition is presented through the Court. At the time of writing, there is a fee of £355 payable. You need to submit an Affidavit of Debt with your petition. An Affidavit is a formal declaration to the Court that the debt is owed to you. An example of an Affidavit is shown on page 131.

If the Court agrees to your petition, it will issue a Bankruptcy Order which places the affairs of your debtor under the Official Receiver. The debtor is required to submit to the Official Receiver a statement detailing all of the assets which he holds and all of the liabilities which he owes. The Official Receiver will contact the creditors and may, if necessary, arrange a creditors' meeting. At this meeting, the creditors can question the debtor, although this is not always necessary. The Official Receiver will then arrange a formal meeting of the creditors after which a decision is made whether the debtor will be made bankrupt. If formal bankruptcy is agreed, then the affairs of the debtor are administered by the Official Receiver whilst he is a bankrupt. If there are sufficient funds, these can be paid to creditors. Each creditor would receive all or part of their debt in 'full and final' settlement of that debt. If all creditors agree, the bankrupt may apply to be discharged from the Bankruptcy Order after settlement. Otherwise, the bankrupt may request to be discharged from the Bankruptcy Order after a number of years, which may be granted with the agreement of the creditors.

AFFIDAVIT OF DEBT
No 4.26 (Rule 4.77)

IN THE HIGH COURT OF JUSTICE **No.** **of 19**

Chancery Division
Companies Court
IN THE MATTER of

AND

IN THE MATTER of The Insolvency Act 1986.

(a) Insert full name, address and description of person making Oath.

I (a) [ ]

MAKE OATH AND SAY AS FOLLOWS :-

(b) Delete as applicable.

(c) State capacity eg director, secretary, solicitor, etc.

(d) State full name and address of Creditor.

1. That [b] [I am a Creditor of the above-named Company] [I am [c]

of (d) [ ]

a Creditor of the above-named Company.
I have been concerned in this matter

(e) State means of knowledge of matters sworn to in Affidavit.

(e) [ ]

and am authorised by the Creditor to make this Affidavit on its/his behalf].

(f) Insert date.

2. That the said Company on [f] the date on which the Company went into liquidation * was and still is justly and truly indebted [to me] [to the said Creditor] in the sum of £ as shown in the proof of debt exhibited hereto marked "A".

Sworn at

this day of

Before me, *Commissioner of Oaths*

*** NOTE:** A company goes into liquidation if it passes a resolution for voluntary winding-up or an order for its winding-up is made by the Court at a time when it has not already gone into liquidation by passing such a resolution

1426

Voluntary Arrangements

Often, an individual is aware that he is unable to meet his debts and can see no way out of the situation. He can apply to the Court to make a Voluntary Arrangement with the creditors. The Court will appoint an authorised Insolvency Practitioner who will administer the affairs of the debtor and request an interim Court Order. This prevents creditors taking further legal action for recovery of debts against the debtor. However, all Voluntary Arrangements with creditors require the creditors' approval to the proposals set out by the debtor. To obtain agreement, the debtor must secure the approval of creditors up to 75% of the value of outstanding debt. If this is agreed, the Insolvency Practitioner will administer payment of the debts. However, the debtor could still be made bankrupt if he fails to meet his obligations under the Voluntary Agreement. The Voluntary Arrangement can be a more advantageous route for creditors as it allows the debtor to continue trading. This gives the possibility that profits generated from trading may enable the debt to be paid.

Administrative Orders

As an alternative to the voluntary arrangement, the Court can issue an Administration Order. This is usually granted where the total amount of debt is below a 'de minimus limit' (currently £5,000). Under an Administration Order, the debtor will pay an agreed amount each month to the Court. The Court will then pay the various creditors on a pro rata basis from these funds. Creditors are not obliged to comply with the Administration Order. They may opt out which leaves them free to pursue their debt independently. However, once again, the Administration Order may result in the debt being paid at an earlier stage because it will allow the debtor to continue trading.

Voluntary Bankruptcy

Finally, your debtor could initiate proceedings himself by declaring to the Court that he is voluntarily bankrupt. Often debtors get fed up with people chasing them for money and decide to place their affairs under the Court's jurisdiction with a Voluntary

Declaration of Bankruptcy. The same procedures are followed as before. An Official Receiver is appointed and the various creditors lodge an official claim with the Receiver. The Court will then decide whether bankruptcy is appropriate or whether alternative arrangements can be agreed.

How to Initiate a Company Liquidation

There are several ways in which a company can be liquidated.

Statutory Demand

A company can be served with a Statutory Demand which requires it to pay it's debts within 21 days. Failure to pay the debt means that you, the creditor, can apply to the Court to wind the company up. This is called a Creditors Petition for Compulsory Liquidation. A sample of a petition for the winding up of a company can be seen on pages 135 to 137. Again, the petition must have a sworn Affidavit of Debt accompanying it, a sample of which can be seen on page 131. You may want to obtain a Confidential Status Report on the company to assess the likelihood of obtaining any funds by way of a distribution from the Official Receiver. An example of such a report on a big company is shown on pages 157 to 161.

The Court will issue a formal Winding Up Order and appoint an Official Receiver to administer the company's affairs. The Official Receiver will draw up a statement of affairs relating to the company which lists it's total assets and total liabilities. The Receiver will then call a meeting of the company's creditors. At this meeting, creditors have an opportunity to ask detailed questions relating to the Statement of Affairs. They will want to know why the company has found itself in an insolvent position. Sometimes, the Official Receiver will investigate the affairs of the company to ensure that the directors have met all their duties properly. If the Official Receiver finds that the directors have been trading fraudulently, they can be disqualified for two years. There is also a possibility that the debts of the company can be made personal debts of the directors.

The Statement of Affairs of the company will show whether you are likely to receive all, or indeed any, of your debt. There may be preferential creditors ahead of you, or other creditors who have their debts secured against the assets of the company. If there is money available for distribution to other creditors, it will usually be shared amongst those creditors pro rata.

Sometimes, a company will voluntarily liquidate itself. This will be done by either a Members Voluntary Liquidation or a Creditors Voluntary Liquidation.

Members Voluntary Liquidation
A Members Voluntary Liquidation generally occurs because of some internal decisions within the company. To achieve such a liquidation, the directors of the company must sign a 'Statement of Solvency'. This statement is a formal declaration that the company has sufficient assets to meet all of its liabilities in full.

Creditors Voluntary Liquidation
A Creditors Voluntary Liquidation can be forced on a company where a creditor believes he may not be paid and requires that the directors of the company sign a Statement of Solvency. If they are unable to sign such a statement, then the directors can be forced to initiate a winding up operation on the company. They will need to draw up a Statement of Affairs and convene a meeting of creditors. At such a meeting of creditors, a Liquidator may be appointed who will then formally wind up the company's affairs. It is illegal for a company to continue trading once it is insolvent.

WINDING UP PETITION

IN THE COUNTY COURT

In the matter of LTD No.

and in the matter of the Insolvency Act 1986

TO COUNTY COURT

The Petition of

1. Limited (hereinafter called 'the company') was incorporated on the 12th July 1993 under the Companies Act 1985

2. The registered office of the company is at

3. The nominal capital of the company is

4. The principal objects for which the company was established are as follows:

   to carry on business as a general commercial company and other objects stated in the Memorandum of Association of the Company.

5.a. The company is indebted to your Petitioner in the sum of £14,778.68, particulars as follows:

Invoice Date		Number	Value	Paid	Balance
1st June	1993	0.2180	2320.63	0.00	2320.63
3rd June	1993	0.2182	181.63	0.00	181.63
3rd June	1993	0.2189	221.02	0.00	221.02
4th June	1993	0.2192	124.55	0.00	124.55
7th June	1993	0.2202	277.54	0.00	277.54
9th June	1993	0.2203	370.71	0.00	370.71
11th June	1993	0.2209	184.25	0.00	184.25
11th June	1993	0.2210	277.30	0.00	277.30
11th June	1993	0.2211	1321.88	0.00	1321.88
14th June	1993	0.2216	142.88	0.00	142.88
18th June	1993	0.2222	32.90	0.00	32.90
18th June	1993	0.2223	139.59	0.00	139.59
18th June	1983	0.2224	116.18	0.00	116.18
18th June	1993	0.2225	72.26	0.00	72.26
18th June	1993	0.2226	74.73	0.00	74.73
21st June	1993	0.2231	446.27	0.00	446.27
22nd June	1993	0.2234	718.91	0.00	718.91
23rd June	1993	0.2237	73.18	0.00	73.18
22nd June	1993	0.2239	88.44	0.00	88.44
28th June	1993	0.2252	222.08	0.00	222.08
30th June	1993	0.2257	371.24	0.00	371.24
2nd July	1993	0.2267	110.45	0.00	110.45
12th July	1993	0.2290	193.24	0.00	193.24
10th July	1993	0.2294	231.24	0.00	231.24
12th July	1993	0.2299	244.40	0.00	244.40
15th July	1993	0.2305	99.64	0.00	99.64
15th July	1993	0.2306	550.60	0.00	550.60
15th July	1993	0.2307	55.55	0.00	55.55
15th July	1993	0.2308	586.62	0.00	586.62
15th July	1993	0.2309	629.45	0.00	629.45
19th July	1993	0.2313	722.91	0.00	722.91
20th July	1993	0.2315	1137.93	0.00	1137.93
20th July	1993	0.2316	116.09	0.00	116.09
22nd July	1993	0.2326	123.26	0.00	123.26
23rd July	1993	0.2334	402.10	0.00	402.10
26th July	1993	0.2339	170.38	0.00	170.38
26th July	1993	0.2340	278.33	0.00	278.33
29th July	1993	0.2349	555.78	0.00	555.78
29th July	1993	0.2350	395.98	0.00	395.98
28th July	1993	0.2351	209.03	0.00	209.03
26th July	1993	0.2341	187.53	0.00	187.53
Total Outstanding			14778.68		

b. On the the Petitioner served on the company a statutory demand pursuant to section 123 of the Insolvency Act 1986. The company has failed to pay money due or secure or compound the debt to your Petitioner's satisfaction

c. The company is insolvent and unable to pay its debts as and when they become due.

6. In the circumstances it is just and equitable that the company should be wound up.

Your Petitioner therefore prays as follows:

1. That Limited may be wound up by the Court under the provision of the insolvency Act 1986 or

2. That such other order may be made as the Court thinks fit.

NOTE: It is intended to serve this Petition on the company.

ENDORSEMENT

This Petition having been presented to the Court on

will be heard at

on:

DATE

TIME

(or as soon thereafter as the Petition can be heard)

The solicitor to the Petitioner is

NAME

ADDRESS

TELEPHONE NO.

REFERENCE

Chapter 13

VAT and Tax Relief for Bad Debts

If the worst comes to the worst, you may not be able to collect the money owed to you. Nevertheless, you may still be able to obtain some measure of relief from VAT and Income Tax. This will go part way to reducing the overall impact of the bad debt. Let's see how to get relief from VAT and Income Tax.

Relief from VAT on Bad Debts

If you are VAT registered and make supplies of goods or services to a customer for which you do not receive payment, you may be in a position to obtain bad debt relief from VAT on the debt that you have incurred. Relief from VAT on bad debts has been available since 1 October 1978. However, the early legislation only provided for relief from VAT where the customer become insolvent. Following a change in the rules in April 1991, VAT relief can now be claimed without the customer becoming formally declared insolvent.

Circumstances in which VAT Bad Debt Relief can be obtained

You are able to claim VAT relief on bad debts providing that all of the following conditions apply.

- The VAT on the bad debt has already been accounted for on your VAT Return and the VAT has been paid to Customs and Excise.
- The goods or services were supplied in exchange for money.
- The bad debt has been written off in your accounts. This means that there must be a record in your accounts to show that the amount has been written off. A VAT Inspector must be able to verify this if he examines your records. We suggest that you establish a separate bad debt account within the records to which such debts are transferred when written off.
- The bad debt has been outstanding for at least six months from the date of supply (prior to 1 April 1993, the waiting period was one year) except in the case of the liquidation or insolvency of the supplier.
- Ownership of the goods or services must have passed to the customer. No relief can be claimed on a contract with a 'romalpa' clause. This reserves title to the goods until payment has been made. However, if goods have been supplied with a retention of a title clause and these goods have not been passed to a third party with title, relief can be claimed provided the retention of title clause is waived.

The customer must have become insolvent. This is established by some form of official confirmation of inability to pay debts, eg bankruptcy or winding up of a company. In the case of a company, the receiver will issue a certificate stating that, in their opinion, there will be no distribution to the creditors.

HM Customs and Excise may require a copy of the tax invoice(s) relating to the supplies on which the bad debt relief is claimed. If a tax invoice has not been issued then some other form of documentation evidencing your supply must be available. Details of the bad debt should be recorded in a bad debt account to show:

- the amount you have written off as a bad debt
- the amount of VAT you are claiming as bad debt relief
- the VAT period in which you have claimed the refund
- the VAT period in which you originally accounted for and paid the VAT
- details of any part payments received for the bad debt
- the name of the customer
- the date and number of the invoice to which the bad debt relates.

The amount of relief available is normally the VAT charged on the supply or supplies relating to the bad debt. If you establish a separate bad debt account within your records, it will be easy to identify these amounts from the records. If you have received part payment of the debt, you can only claim the VAT amount that is still outstanding.

Let's consider the following examples.

Example 15

Toobie Fore have an account with Bill Overdeux and Co Ltd. Bill Overdeux and Co Ltd went into liquidation on 31 October 1995. Toobie Fore have received a certificate from the Receiver stating no distribution would be available to creditors. The sales ledger account for Toobie Fore shows the following information:

Toobie Fore Sales Ledger Account With Bill Overdeux & Co Ltd

		£			£
1.8.95	Balance B/fwd	14000	31.8.95	Cheque July A/c	14000
15.8.95	1 Timber (incl VAT)	18000	15.9.95	Cheque – Payment on account	15000
16.9.95	2 Bricks (incl VAT)	19000	31.10.95	Balance C/Fwd	44000
22.9.95	3 Goods (Zero rate)	22000			
		73000			73000
31.10.95	Balance	**44000**			

The Bad Debt Relief due will be as follows:

Total due from Bill Overdeux & Co Ltd = £44,000
Comprising:

	Gross	VAT
	£	£
Invoice No 3	22000	
Invoice No 2	19000	2829.78
Invoice No 1	3000	446.80
	44000	**3276.58**

Note VAT on Invoice No 1 is £18,000 x 7/47 = £2,680.85

Proportion $\frac{3000}{18000}$ x £2680.85 = £446.80

The total VAT to be reclaimed by Toobie Fore is £3,276.58

The following example shows how to work out bad debt relief where there are mutual debts.

Example 16

Toobie Fore had made a supply of sand and gravel to Bodgit the Builder. The total supply amounted to £600 plus VAT of £105, giving a total amount of £705 including VAT.

Toobie Fore decide to write off the bad debt but, at the time of writing off the bad debt, they owed Bodgit the Builder £200 plus VAT of £35 for some building work they had completed for them.

The amount Toobie Fore could claim by way of bad debt relief would be £105 being the VAT on their invoice less £35 being the amount of VAT they owe to Bodgit the Builder, giving total VAT relief of £70.

What Happens if Payment is Received after Claiming Bad Debt Relief?

If, after claiming a refund of VAT on a bad debt, you receive payment for the supplies then the VAT on the amount subsequently recovered must be repaid to HM Customs and Excise. This is done by simply adding the VAT on the debt recovered to the total amount of the VAT due in the VAT period in which the debt is recovered.

If you are insured against bad debts, and the insurance is for the VAT inclusive amount of the bad debt, you may claim this amount even though you have received bad debt relief from Customs and Excise.

A Note On Cash Accounting

The cash accounting scheme allows all registered businesses who have an annual turnover below £350,000 to account for VAT on the basis of payments received and made instead of tax invoices issued and received. This means that these businesses automatically receive bad debt relief on outstanding invoices without having to wait for the statutory period of six months.

Further information concerning relief from VAT on bad debts can be obtained from VAT leaflet 700/18/91, available from your local VAT office.

Income Tax Relief for Bad Debts

Bad debt relief for Income Tax purposes is obtained by including the bad debt within the accounts of the business. A provision for bad debts will appear in the profit and loss account as an overhead expense of the business. This will obviously reduce the overall net profit assessable to tax. Income Tax relief may also be available for *doubtful* debts, the Inland Revenue's interpretation of which is discussed below.

The deduction for bad or doubtful debts is made in arriving at the net profit of the year in which the debts become bad or doubtful. Where a deduction is made for doubtful debts, this is generally referred to as a *reserve* for bad debts. Where there is more than one debt included within this reserve, the Inland Revenue ask that the reserve is based on a reasonably accurate valuation of each doubtful debt.

The Inland Revenue will also accept a provision for bad debts after the accounting year ends providing there is evidence that the debt will be bad or doubtful prior to finalisation of the accounts. The Inland Revenue have recently clarified the circumstances where this provision will be allowed. These are:

- a debt existed at the balance sheet date, *and*
- the creditor at that date had no reason to believe that he would not be paid, *but*
- before the accounts were finalised, he discovered that the financial position of the debtor at the balance sheet date was such that, even at that time, he was unlikely to be paid.

For example, a debt may be owed at the end of the accounting year but the debtor may go into administration or liquidation shortly after the accounting year end but before finalisation of the accounts by the accountant.

There is no statutory period beyond which relief for bad debts can be claimed as there is for VAT purposes. Whether a bad or doubtful debt is claimable is a matter of circumstance and fact. The length of time a debt is outstanding is, on it's own, not sufficient grounds for claiming relief.

Indeed, where an Inspector of Taxes is not satisfied that the deduction claimed for bad or doubtful debts is valid, he will need to establish for each individual debt:

- how the extent of its doubtfulness was evaluated
- when this was done
- by whom

- what information was used in arriving at the evaluation that the debt was bad or doubtful.

Therefore, in order to approve a bad debt claim, the Inspector may require sight of all the evidence available. This may include copies of correspondence with the debtor and third parties concerning the debt, eg solicitors, banks, factoring agencies etc, together with any reports that have been obtained regarding the financial status of the debtor. In addition, the Inspector may wish to see copies of any internal correspondence such as memos and minutes of meetings at which the debt may have been discussed. It is essential that all evidence concerning the ways in which you have sought to recover your debts is preserved, in case the Inspector wants to see them. If you don't have an efficient credit control system, you may find it hard to obtain relief for bad or doubtful debts simply because you cannot supply the evidence that you have tried to collect the debt.

If a bad debt is subsequently recovered, you can enter the amount received as a trading receipt of the accounting period when the money was paid to you.

If you are exposed to bad or doubtful debts, consult your accountant so that a provision can be made in your accounts for the bad debt. Also make available to your accountant any information which will help him to convince the Taxman of your valid claim.

Appendix 1

Model Answers

Answer to Exercise 1 Page 4

	Before	After 5% price rise	After 5% price cut
	£	£	£
Value of Sales	10000	10500	9500
Total Costs	8000	8000	8000
Profit	2000	2500	1500
% Change in Profit	-	+25%	-25%

Conclusion: A 10% change in prices can produce a 50% change in profits.

Answer to Exercise 2 Page 8

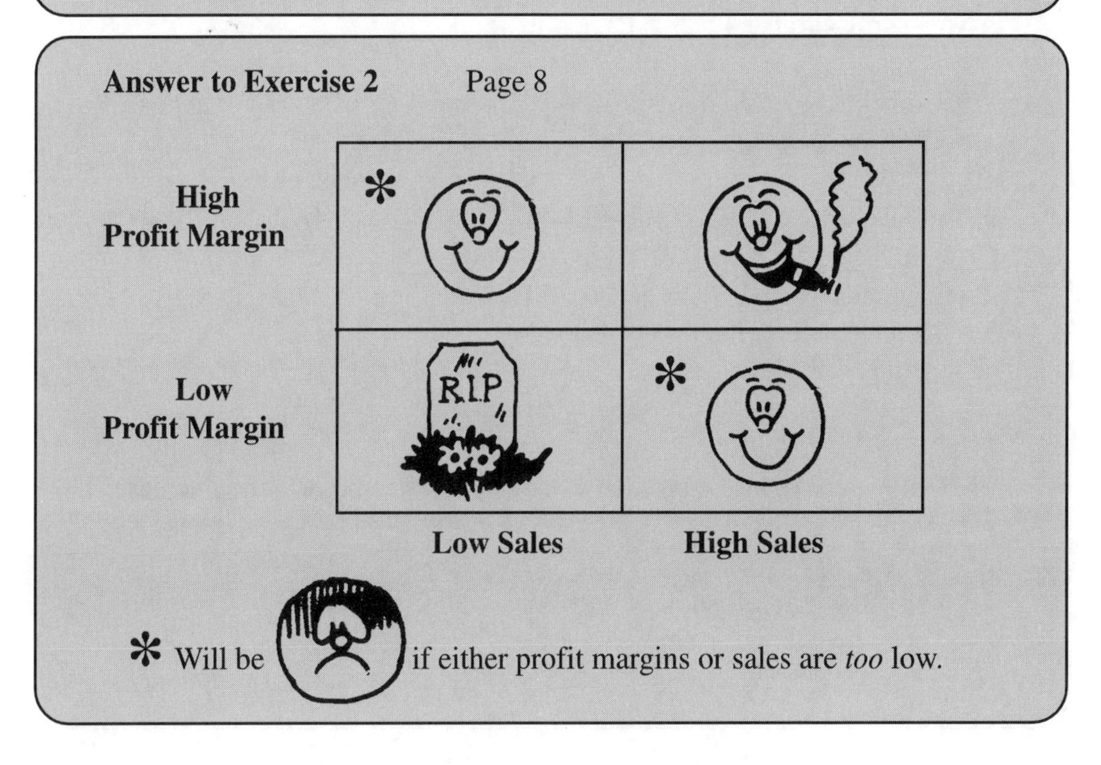

Answer to Exercise 3 Page 39

1 Each ice cream costs 12p and sells for 22p. The fixed costs are £50. Therefore:

$$\text{Break-even Quantity} = \frac{\text{Fixed Costs}}{\text{Selling Price} - \text{Unit Cost}}$$

$$\text{Break-even Quantity} = \frac{£50}{22p - 12p} = 500$$

2 Once the break-even point has been reached, all additional sales generate pure profit. If each ice cream has a profit of 10p then you need to sell 200 ice creams on top of the 500 needed to break even. Therefore, you need to sell 700 ice creams to produce a profit of £20.

Answer to Exercise 4 Page 45

We will begin by calculating Fred's cost per mile on each item of expense as follows.

	£	pence per mile
Diesel/Oil	1900	4.75
Driver's Salary	3750	9.37
Tax/Insurance	1200	3.00
Servicing/Repairs	500	1.25
Depreciation of Vehicle	1500	3.75
	8850	22.12

The following expenses are fixed which means that they will not increase with the extra mileage.

Driver's Salary, Tax/Insurance and Depreciation of Vehicle

Continued

Answer to Exercise 4 (Contd)

This means that the cost of every extra mile run would be:

	Cost per Mile (pence)
Diesel/Oil	4.75
Servicing/Repairs	1.25
	6.00

Provided Fred quotes a price in excess of 6 pence per mile, he will make additional profit. Of course, if Fred can win the bid at his normal rates (which were originally based on costs including fixed costs), he will make a *handsome* profit.

Answer to Exercise 5 Page 53

First calculate the fixed costs as:

Product X	1/3 x 36,000	=	12,000
Product Y	1/3 x 38,000	=	12,667
Product Z	1/3 x 34,000	=	11,333
Total Fixed Costs			36,000

Rearranging the operating statement in marginal costing format produces:

	ProdX	**ProdY**	**ProdZ**	**Total**
	£	£	£	£
Sales	32000	50000	45000	127000
less Variable Costs	24000	25333	22667	72000
Contribution	8000	24667	22333	55000
less Fixed Costs	(12000)	(12667)	(11333)	36000
Net Profit	(4000)	12000	11000	19000

Continued overleaf

Answer to Exercise 5 (Contd)

From this, it will be seen that product X produces a contribution of £8,000. If it were dropped, the position would be:

	£
Contribution Product X	24667
Contribution Product Y	22333
Combined Contribution	47000
less Fixed Costs	36000
Net Profit	11000

Thus, dropping product X reduces total profits by £8,000 so product X should not be dropped until a more profitable replacement can be found.

Other factors which need to be considered include:

- Although product X provides some contribution, it is not very much. Alternative, more profitable products or markets should be considered.

- We have assumed that the fixed costs were of a general nature which would remain even if product X was dropped. If dropping product X did result in the elimination of some fixed costs then there may be a case for dropping product X. However, this is unlikely given the very nature of fixed costs.

Exercise 6 Page 67

Sale Price of Goods £	Cost of Goods £	Lost Profit %	Add Sales to Cover debt
500	475	5	10,000
1000	900	10	10,000
3000	2550	15	20,000
5000	4000	20	25,000

Exercise 7 Page 70

1 Computation of annual interest rate:

$$5 \times \frac{365}{55} = 33\%$$

2 The discount of 5% is not profitable to Toobie Fore. As they are paying 12% on their borrowing and the annual interest rate on the discount is 33%, they are better off waiting 60 days for their money and not offering any discount.

Exercise 8 Pages 94, 95 and 96

Profit Forecast From May 1996 to April 1997

	ACTUAL 1994/95		ACTUAL 1995/96		BUDGET 1996/97		BUDGET BY MONTH											
							MAY	JUN	JUL	AUG	SEP	OCT	NOV	DEC	JAN	FEB	MAR	APR
	£	%	£	%	£	%	£	£	£	£	£	£	£	£	£	£	£	£
GROSS PROFIT B/fwd	34000	43	42700	44	57005	49	3270	3270	3270	7449	3270	3270	3270	16855	3271	3270	3270	3270
VARIABLE OVERHEADS																		
Staff Wages	3400	4	4270	4	5785	5	336	336	336	858	336	336	336	1571	335	335	335	335
FIXED OVERHEADS																		
Rent	6000	8	6000	6	6000	5	500	500	500	500	500	500	500	500	500	500	500	500
Rates	3000	4	3200	3	3600	3	300	300	300	300	300	300	300	300	300	300	300	300
Light and Heat	3000	4	3100	3	3255	3	272	272	272	271	271	271	271	271	271	271	271	271
Office Salaries	1250	2	1500	2	1800	2	150	150	150	150	150	150	150	150	150	150	150	150
Advertising	400	1	600	1	1200	1	100	100	100	100	100	100	100	100	100	100	100	100
Motor Expenses	1560	2	2080	2	2400	2	200	200	200	200	200	200	200	200	200	200	200	200
Telephone	200	1	350	1	480	0	40	40	40	40	40	40	40	40	40	40	40	40
Sundries	150	0	225	0	300	0	25	25	25	25	25	25	25	25	25	25	25	25
TOTAL FIXED OVERHEADS	15560	22	17055	18	19035	16	1587	1587	1587	1586	1586	1586	1586	1586	1586	1586	1586	1586
NET PROFIT	15040	19	21375	22	32185	28	1347	1347	1347	5005	5005	1348	1348	13698	1350	1349	1349	1349

Exercise 9 Page 95

Calculation of average debt outstanding November

Debts outstanding November £45,250

Annual Sales £290,000

Average debt outstanding

$$\frac{45250}{290000} \times 365 = 57 \text{ Days}$$

We can see that, during November, the average debt outstanding has increased from 53 days to 57 days.

Comment: From looking at the aged debtor analysis, we can see that the total debts outstanding at the end of the month have increased from £42,000 during October to £45,250.

Importantly, the debts outstanding for over three months have increased from £1,500 to £12,250.

Most notable is Customer 4 who still has not paid the total debt which was outstanding at the end of October and, indeed, Toobie Fore have made additional credit sales to the customer in the sum of £4,000. Given the customer's reluctance to pay previous invoices, Toobie Fore should have refused to allow any further credit and should either have refused to make further supplies to the customer until the previous invoices were settled, or have insisted on cash on delivery.

Toobie Fore need to keep a very careful eye on their credit control as the proportion of debtors over three months old is rising, this indicates a need to get tough with certain customers.

Exercise 10 Page 99

Debtors Turnover Ratio

	1 Mth	2 Mths	3 Mths	3 Mths+	Totals
November	30000	3000		12250	45250
December	16000	10000	2000	2000	30000

Average Debtors: 45250
30000
75250 ÷ 2 = 37625

Debtors Turnover Ratio $\frac{290000}{37625} = 7.70$

Average Collection Period $\frac{365}{7.70} = 47.40$ Days

The average collection period for December has decreased from 55 days to 47 days. Obviously, Toobie Fore's credit control procedures are proving successful. However, the average collection period is still too high so they will still need to see if there are ways to decrease this figure further.

Answer to Exercise 11 Pages 120 to 122

The total debt to be sought by Toobie Fore would be as follows:

	£
Total Debt Outstanding	587.50
Court Costs	60.00
Oral examination costs	30.00
Total	**677.50**

It would appear from the answers to the various questions that probably due to Mr Toupe's recent house purchase, his overall financial position is not particularly healthy.

A Warrant of Execution would probably not be appropriate as all of his tangible personal assets would appear to be under some form of HP agreement. Mr Toupe does, however, have an investment account with the XX Building Society, the current balance on which is in excess of the total debt plus costs owed. Given this, it may be appropriate to apply for a Garnishee Order to be issued on a Building Society account to recover the debt. However, in the interim period, as the Garnishee Order applies to the account at the day the Order is served, Mr Toupe may have removed funds from this account. If so, the secondary action which you may wish to take could involve a Charging Order as Mr Toupe does have £15,000 equity in his property. It is likely that such an Order would be effective as it would probably force Mr Toupe to pay as he is unlikely to allow you to apply to the Court to sell his house for such a small debt. However, in the event you did need to apply to the Court to sell the house under the Order, of course the outstanding mortgage on the property would need to be satisfied first.

Appendix 2

CONFIDENTIAL STATUS REPORT

SUPPLIED BY
FCC CREDIT MANAGEMENT
(A DIVISION OF FCC MANAGEMENT SERVICES LTD)
REGISTERED IN ENGLAND No 1766258
FEDERATION HOUSE 1 THE BRIARS
WATERBERRY DRIVE WATERLOOVILLE,
PORTSMOUTH HANTS PO7 7YH
TEL: (01705) 232113
FAX: (01705) 232126

SAMPLE ENHANCED REPORT

Date:-	Date of Report
Our Ref:-	AB0513/014/01
Your Ref:-	6609

For the attention of The Client

SERVICE REQUESTED

This report is issued in response to your Status enquiry and in respect of your proposed credit figure of £5,000 – £5,500 to extend credit.

SUBJECT IDENTIFICATION AND LOCATION

CORRECT REGISTERED NAME:	A COMPANY LIMITED
REGISTERED NUMBER:	1234567
TRADING NAMES USED:	None
REGISTERED OFFICE:	Any Industrial Estate, Anytown, Anyshire, AAl lAA.
PRINCIPAL TRADING ADDRESS:	As Registered Office
TELEPHONE NUMBER:	0121 123 1234
OTHER TRADING LOCATIONS:	None

COMPANY STRUCTURE AND OWNERSHIP

DATE OF INCORPORATION:	21st May 1971
PREVIOUS NAMES:	The company was incorporated under the present day style.

CONFIDENTIAL STATUS REPORT

SUPPLIED BY
FCC CREDIT MANAGEMENT
(A DIVISION OF FCC MANAGEMENT SERVICES LTD)
REGISTERED IN ENGLAND No 1766258
FEDERATION HOUSE 1 THE BRIARS
WATERBERRY DRIVE WATERLOOVILLE,
PORTSMOUTH HANTS PO7 7YH
TEL: (01705) 232113
FAX: (01705) 232126

CAPITALISATION:
The nominal share capital of the company is £2,000 divided into ordinary £1 shares. 1,600 shares have been issued as follows:- 2 shares have been issued subject to payment wholly in cash and the remainder for other considerations.

DIRECTORS	SHAREHOLDING	OTHER DIRECTORSHIPS
Mr Smith, 35, Any Street, Anytown, Anyshire, AAl 1AA.	0	Smith Trading Ltd
Mrs Smith, (Address as above)	0	Smith Trading Ltd

COMPANY SECRETARY:	Mrs Sharp	
OTHER SHAREHOLDERS:	Smith Trading Ltd	1,280 shares
	Jones Co Ltd	320
SUBSIDIARIES:	None	

FINANCIAL DETAILS
ANNUAL RETURN DATE: 19th September 1991

REGISTERED INDEBTEDNESS:
The companies registered indebtedness in respect of mortgages, charges and debentures at the annual return date was not disclosed.

MORTGAGES AND CHARGES:
There are 3 outstanding charges recorded on the Mortgage Register including a Legal Charge created 20th July 1992 in favour of Midland Bank Plc securing all monies due or to become due to the Bank.

BANKERS:
Midland Bank Plc,
The High Street
Anytown
Anyshire
Sort Code:- 01-01-01

It is agreed that all information is furnished for your private use only and is supplied in confidence. The client agrees with the Agency that all such information is supplied on the express understanding that the Agency is not held responsible for damage or loss arising from insufficient or inaccurate information furnished to the Client whether by reason of mistake or negligence of the Agency or its Servants

CONSUMER CREDIT LICENCE No 339486

CONFIDENTIAL STATUS REPORT

SUPPLIED BY
FCC CREDIT MANAGEMENT
(A DIVISION OF FCC MANAGEMENT SERVICES LTD)
REGISTERED IN ENGLAND No 1766258
FEDERATION HOUSE 1 THE BRIARS
WATERBERRY DRIVE WATERLOOVILLE,
PORTSMOUTH HANTS PO7 7YH
TEL: (01705) 232113
FAX: (01705) 232126

ACCOUNTING EXTRACTS:

YEAR ENDED	31 March 1991	31 March 1990
TURNOVER	Not stated	Not stated
PROFIT / LOSS (after tax)		
FIXED ASSETS	64,701	57,015
CURRENT ASSETS	145,257	142,702
CURRENT LIABILITIES	81,594	91,059
NET CURRENT ASSETS	63,663	51,643
P & L ACCOUNT (DEFICIT)	85,586	65,880
NET WORTH	103,264	83,558

COMMENTS:
The company has exercised its rights under the Companies Act 1985 to file modified accounts which precludes the need to file Profit & Loss Account or Director's Report, therefore turnover and profit figures have not been disclosed. However, it is possible to estimate the company's profitability by movements in profit and loss account reserves which would indicate from the information available that a profit has been made of £19,706.

Overall, the company has maintained a satisfactory level of profitability and growth over the years, the Balance Sheet figures quoted above being typical of past years' operating Statements. At 31st March 1991, liquid funds were seen to increase to £63,663 allowing the company sufficient funds with which to discharge any short-term commitments they may have in existence. Accumulated Reserves were recorded as £85,586, the overall Net Worth of the enterprise meanwhile, increasing to £103,264 of which £16,078 was attributable to a Revaluation Reserve taken on the company's Freehold premises.

Bank Overdraft facilities rose marginally throughout the period from £31,098 in 1990 to £35,278, and are secured by way of a Fixed & Floating Charge on all the Assets of the company. The company has provided for Liabilities and Charges, ie: deferred taxation of £2,100.

The company's Auditors, Cole and Cole Ltd, Any Street, Anytown, Anyshire were seen to hand in their resignation on the 10th May, stating that there were no circumstances connected with this which would need to be brought to the attention of either the members or creditors of the company. The company now employ SJ Lindsey & Co of Main Street, Nexttown, Nextshire, to handle their affairs.

It is agreed that all information is furnished for your private use only and is supplied in confidence. The client agrees with the Agency that all such information is supplied on the express understanding that the Agency is not held responsible for damage or loss arising from insufficient or inaccurate information furnished to the Client whether by reason of mistake or negligence of the Agency or its Servants

CONSUMER CREDIT LICENCE No 339486

CONFIDENTIAL STATUS REPORT

SUPPLIED BY
FCC CREDIT MANAGEMENT
(A DIVISION OF FCC MANAGEMENT SERVICES LTD)
REGISTERED IN ENGLAND No 1766258
FEDERATION HOUSE 1 THE BRIARS
WATERBERRY DRIVE WATERLOOVILLE,
PORTSMOUTH HANTS PO7 7YH
TEL: (01705) 232113
FAX: (01705) 232126

During a recent interview held with Mrs Smith at the heading address, she confirmed that no major events have occurred within the company's overall structure or funding since the last audited Statements were prepared. Mrs Smith added that the company regard Smith Trading Ltd, who operate from the Registered Office Address as their parent company. This company is also wholly owned by the two principals of the company. Mrs Smith reported that she was awarded Businesswoman of the year in 1987, a superb achievement of which she is very proud to have held. It was also reported that payments to suppliers etc are currently slow, however, a recent meeting with the company's Auditors today, has reassured her that they have no concern whatsoever regarding the company's ability to continue trading actively and see the recession through. Mrs Smith states that the company have the continued support of their Bankers if required, and whilst the year to March 1992 was difficult, it is believed a break-even position will be shown at period end when accounts become accessible. The current trading position of the company is said to be extremely busy with order books being at a high level.

BACKGROUND AND OPERATIONAL DETAILS

PRINCIPAL ACTIVITIES:
The company is principally engaged in the business of Manufacturing Mixers and Ancillary Plant.

EMPLOYEES: The company employs an average of 7 full-time and 1 part-time people.

PREMISES:
The company trades from rented premises at the heading address which comprises Industrial Unit.

TRADE EXPOSURE:
During a recent interview, Mrs Smith was reluctant to furnish any existing trade suppliers in order to gain comments upon other trade accounts and the manner in which they are handled. This is believed to be due to her previous comments made that most creditors are being paid a little late in excess of terms.

It is agreed that all information is furnished for your private use only and is supplied in confidence. The client agrees with the Agency that all such information is supplied on the express understanding that the Agency is not held responsible for damage or loss arising from insufficient or inaccurate information furnished to the Client whether by reason of mistake or negligence of the Agency or its Servants

CONSUMER CREDIT LICENCE No 339486

CONFIDENTIAL STATUS REPORT

SUPPLIED BY
FCC CREDIT MANAGEMENT
(A DIVISION OF FCC MANAGEMENT SERVICES LTD)
REGISTERED IN ENGLAND No 1766258
FEDERATION HOUSE 1 THE BRIARS
WATERBERRY DRIVE WATERLOOVILLE,
PORTSMOUTH HANTS PO7 7YH
TEL: (01705) 232113
FAX: (01705) 232126

CONCLUSION:

In answer to your enquiry of recent, A Company Ltd have a pleasing past trading history on file and we can see no reason why this level of activity should not continue in the foreseeable future. We can see no visible cause why your proposed credit figure of £5,000 – £5,500 should not prove suitable for your purposes.

It is agreed that all information is furnished for your private use only and is supplied in confidence. The client agrees with the Agency that all such information is supplied on the express understanding that the Agency is not held responsible for damage or loss arising from insufficient or inaccurate information furnished to the Client whether by reason of mistake or negligence of the Agency or its Servants

CONSUMER CREDIT LICENCE No 339486

CONFIDENTIAL STATUS REPORT

SUPPLIED BY
FCC CREDIT MANAGEMENT
(A DIVISION OF FCC MANAGEMENT SERVICES LTD)
REGISTERED IN ENGLAND No 1766258
FEDERATION HOUSE 1 THE BRIARS
WATERBERRY DRIVE WATERLOOVILLE,
PORTSMOUTH HANTS PO7 7YH
TEL: (01705) 232113
FAX: (01705) 232126

SAMPLE BUSINESS-NAME REPORT

Our ref:- AB0303/0005/03
Your Ref:- 687151/DH
Date : Date of report

SUBJECT **SOME FURNITURE CENTRE**

SERVICE REQUESTED
This report is issued in response to your non-limited status enquiry dated 3 March 1993 and in respect of your proposed credit figure of £25,316.

CORRECT TRADING STYLE As above

TRADING ADDRESS
Unit 2
Any Road
Anytown
Anyshire
AA1 1AA

TELEPHONE LISTING 0123 456789

LEGAL STATUS
The subject is a non-limited concern operating under the ownership and control of a father and son partnership, Mr K something and Mr B something.

PRINCIPAL ACTIVITIES AND NUMBER OF EMPLOYEES
The business is principally engaged in that of retailing carpets and bedding. It was commented that furniture could be acquired if requested by the customer. The only other employees, other than the partners are 4 contract workers, although more would be 'taken on' if there was a heavy work load.

It is agreed that all information is furnished for your private use only and is supplied in confidence. The client agrees with the Agency that all such information is supplied on the express understanding that the Agency is not held responsible for damage or loss arising from insufficient or inaccurate information furnished to the Client whether by reason of mistake or negligence of the Agency or its Servants

CONSUMER CREDIT LICENCE No 339486

CONFIDENTIAL STATUS REPORT

SUPPLIED BY
FCC CREDIT MANAGEMENT
(A DIVISION OF FCC MANAGEMENT SERVICES LTD)
REGISTERED IN ENGLAND No 1766258
FEDERATION HOUSE 1 THE BRIARS
WATERBERRY DRIVE WATERLOOVILLE,
PORTSMOUTH HANTS PO7 7YH
TEL: (01705) 232113
FAX: (01705) 232126

DATE ESTABLISHED AND PERIOD AT ADDRESS

The business was established during 1970, but has only operated from the above address for the past 10 years.

ACCOMMODATION AND LOCATION

It was reported that the premises are leased and offers office, workshop and showroom facilities; the area of which is not known.

BRANCH ADDRESS

There are no further branches relating to this concern.

TRADE EXPOSURES

Two trade suppliers were contacted on your behalf, the first of which reported that dealings have been in existence for 8 years, with a credit limit of £7,000 per month set on the account. The average exposures were not revealed, although, previously up to the credit limit has been taken at one time. Terms offered are 20th MFI, and payment is always prompt.

The second trade reference stated that dealings have been in duration for the past 3 years, and that the average amount of credit taken each month is £500. Terms offered on the account are 30 days and payment is always within the given time.

BANKERS — Lloyds Bank plc
Sort Code:- 00-00-00

It is agreed that all information is furnished for your private use only and is supplied in confidence. The client agrees with the Agency that all such information is supplied on the express understanding that the Agency is not held responsible for damage or loss arising from insufficient or inaccurate information furnished to the Client whether by reason of mistake or negligence of the Agency or its Servants

CONSUMER CREDIT LICENCE No 339486

CONFIDENTIAL STATUS REPORT

SUPPLIED BY
FCC CREDIT MANAGEMENT
(A DIVISION OF FCC MANAGEMENT SERVICES LTD)
REGISTERED IN ENGLAND No 1766258
FEDERATION HOUSE 1 THE BRIARS
WATERBERRY DRIVE WATERLOOVILLE,
PORTSMOUTH HANTS PO7 7YH
TEL: (01705) 232113
FAX: (01705) 232126

LITIGATION

A search made of public records information has shown nothing of a detrimental nature recorded against the subject.

ADDITIONAL INFORMATION

During the recent interview with Mr K Something the details contained in this report were confirmed, and he further stated that business is quite good. Mr something commented that the end of the financial year is 31 July and that the turnover at the end of the period, should be greater than the end of the previous year. He declined to supply any figures to uphold this statement.

CONCLUSION

Although Mr Something was very helpful, because of the lack of financial figure 5 from which we could ascertain the trading levels and profitability of the business, we would be unable to recommend the credit figure requested. We would advise that all dealings be restricted to £5,000.

CONSUMER CREDIT LICENCE No 339486

Admission

When to fill in this form

- Only fill in this form if you are admitting all or some of the claim **and** you are asking for time to pay
- If you are disputing the claim or you wish to pay the amount claimed, read the back of the summons

How to fill in this form

- Tick the correct boxes and give as much information as you can. **Then sign and date the form.**
- Make the offer of payment in box 11 on the back of this form. **If you make no offer the plaintiff will decide how you should pay.**
- You can get help to complete this form at **any** county court office or citizens? advice bureau.

Where to send this form

- **If you admit the claim in full**
  Send the completed form to the address shown at box (2) on the front of the summons. If there is no address in box (2) send the form to the address in box (1).
- **If you admit only part of the claim**
  Send the form **to the court** at the address given on the summons, together with the white defence form (N9B)

What happens next

- **If you admit the claim in full and offer to pay**
  If the plaintiff accepts your offer, judgement will be entered and you will be sent an order telling you how and when to pay. If the plaintiff does **not** accept your offer, the court will fix a rate of payment based on the details you have given in this form and the plaintiff?s comments. Judgement will be entered and you will be sent an order telling you how and when to pay.
- **If you admit only part of the claim**
  The court will tell you what to do next.

How much of the claim do you admit?

☐ I admit the full amount claimed as shown on the summons **or**

☐ I admit the amount of £

1 Personal Details

Surname

Forename

☐ Mr ☐ Mrs ☐ Miss ☐ Ms

☐ Married ☐ Single ☐ Other *(specify)*

Age

Address

Postcode

In the County Court

Case Number *Always quote this*

Plaintiff *(including ref.)*

Defendant

2 Dependants *(people you look after financially)*

Number of children in each age group

under 11 ☐ 11-15 ☐ 16-17 ☐ 18 & over ☐

Other dependants *(give details)*

3 Employment

☐ **I am employed as a**

My employer is

Jobs other than main job *(give details)*

☐ **I am self employed as a**

Annual turnover is.............................. £

☐ **I am not** in arrears with my national insurance contributions, income tax and VAT

☐ **I am** in arrears and I owe............. £

Give details of:
(a) contracts and other work in hand

(b) any sums due for work done

☐ **I have been unemployed for** years months

☐ **I am a pensioner**

4 Bank accounts and savings

☐ **I have a bank account**

☐ The account is in credit by....... £

☐ The account is overdrawn by.... £

☐ **I have a savings or building society account**

The amount in the account is......... £

5 Property

I live in ☐ my own property ☐ lodgings

☐ jointly owned property ☐ council property

☐ rented property

N9A Form of admission and statement of means to accompany Form N1 (order 9, rule2) (1.95) N9A 172 *Printed by Satellite Press Limited*

6 Income

My usual take home pay *(including overtime, commission, bonuses etc)*	£ per
Income support	£ per
Child benefit(s)	£ per
Other state benefit(s)	£ per
My pension(s)	£ per
Others living in my home give me	£ per
Other income *(give details below)*	
	£ per
	£ per
	£ per
Total income	**£ per**

7 Expenses

(Do not include any payments made by other members of the household out of their own income)

I have regular expenses as follows:

Mortgage *(including second mortgage)*	£ per
Rent	£ per
Council Tax	£ per
Gas	£ per
Electricity	£ per
Water charges	£ per
TV rental and licence	£ per
HP repayments	£ per
Mail order	£ per
Housekeeping, food, school meals	£ per
Travelling expenses	£ per
Children?s clothing	£ per
Maintenance payments	£ per
Others *(not court orders or credit debts listed in boxes 9 and 10)*	
	£ per
	£ per
	£ per
Total expenses	**£ per**

8 Priority debts

(This section is for arrears only. Do not include regular expenses listed in box 7.)

Rent arrears	£ per
Mortgage arrears	£ per
Council Tax/Community Charge arrears	£ per
Water charges arrears	£ per
Fuel depts: Gas	£ per
Electricity	£ per
Other	£ per
Maintenance arrears	£ per
Others *(give details below)*	
	£ per
	£ per
Total priority debts	**£ per**

9 Court orders

Court	Case No.	
		£ per
Total court order instalments		**£ per**

Of the payments above, I am behind with payments to *(please list)*

10 Credit debts

Loans and credit card debts *(please list)*

	£ per
	£ per
	£ per

Of the payments above, I am behind with payments to *(please list)*

11 Do you wish to make an offer of payment?

- *If you take away the total of boxes 7, 8 and 9 and the payments you are making in box 10 from the total in box 6 you will get some idea of the sort of sum you should offer. The offer you make should be one you can afford.*

☐ I can pay the amount admitted on

or

☐ I can pay by monthly instalments of £

12 Declaration

I declare that the details I have given above are true to the best of my knowledge

Signed **Dated**

Position *(firm or company)*

Defence and Counterclaim

When to fill in this form

- Only fill in this form if you wish to dispute all or part of the claim **and/or** make a claim against the plaintiff (counterclaim).

How to fill in this form

- Please check that the correct case details are shown on this form. You must ensure that all boxes at the top right of this form are completed. You can obtain the correct names and numbers from the summons. The court cannot trace your case without this information.
- Follow the instructions given in each section. Tick the correct boxes and give the other details asked for.
- If you wish only to make a claim against the plaintiff (counterclaim) go to section 5.
- Complete and sign section 6 before returning this form.

Where to send this form

- Send or take this form immediately to the court office at the address shown above.
- If you admit part of the claim and you are asking for time to pay, you will also need to fill in the blue admission form (N9A) and send **both** reply forms to the court.
- Keep the summons and a copy of this defence; you may need them

What happens next

- You may be entitled to legal aid. Ask about the legal aid scheme at any county court office, Citizens Advice Bureau, legal advice centre or firm of solicitors displaying the legal aid sign.

What happens next

- If you complete box 3 on this form, the court will ask the plaintiff to confirm that he has received payment. If he tells the court that you have not paid, the court will tell you what you should do.
- If you complete box 4 or 5, the court will tell you what you should do.
- If the summons is not from your local county court, it will automatically be transferred to your local court.

1 How much of the claim do you dispute?

☐ **I dispute the full amount claimed** *(go to section 2)*

or

☐ **I admit the amount of** £ ________

If you dispute only part of the claim you must **either**:

- pay the amount admitted to the person named at the address for payment in box (2) on the front of the summons or if there is no address in box (2), send the money to the address in box (1) (see How to Pay on the back of the summons). Then send this defence to the court.

or

- complete the blue admission form and this defence form and send them to the court.

Tick whichever applies

☐ I paid the amount admitted on *(date)* ________

or

☐ I enclose the completed form of admission

(go to section 2)

In the	**County Court**
Case Number *Always quote this*	
Plaintiff *(including ref.)*	
Defendant	

The court office is open from 10 am to 4 pm Monday to Friday

2 Arbitration under the small claims procedure

How the claim will be dealt with if defended

If the total the plaintiff is claiming is £3,000 or less, it will be dealt with by arbitration (small claims procedure) unless the court decides the case is too difficult to be dealt with in this informal way. Costs and the grounds for setting aside an arbitration award are strictly limited. If the claim is not dealt with by arbitration, costs, including the costs of help from a legal representative, may be allowed.

If the total the plaintiff is claiming is more than £3,000, it can still be dealt with by arbitration if you or the plaintiff ask for it and the court approves. If your claim is dealt with by arbitration in these circumstances, costs may be allowed.

Please tick this box if you would like the claim dealt with by arbitration. ☐

(go to section 3)

3 Do you dispute this claim because you have already paid it? *Tick whichever applies*

☐ **No** *(go to section 4)*

☐ **Yes I paid** £ ________ **to the plaintiff**

on ________ *(before the summons was issued - see summons)*

Give details of where and how you paid it in the box below *(then go to section 6)*

Printed by Satellite Press Limited

Case No.

4 If you dispute the claim for reasons other than payment, what are your reasons?

Use the box below to give full details *(If you need to continue on a separate sheet, put the case number in the top right hand corner)*

5 If you wish to make a claim against the plaintiff (counterclaim)

If your claim is for a specific sum of money, how much are you asking? £

- If your claim against the plaintiff is for more than the plaintiff's claim against you, you may have to pay a fee. Ask at your local court office whether a fee is payable.
- You may not be able to make a counterclaim where the plaintiff is the Crown (eg a Government Department). Ask at your local county court office for further information.

What are your reasons for making the counterclaim?

- Use the box opposite to give full details. *(If you need to continue on a separate sheet, put the case number in the top right hand corner.)*

(go on to section 6)

1 Signed *(To be signed by you or by your solicitor)*

Position *(If signing on behalf of firm or company)*

Dated

Give an address to which notices about this case can be sent to you

Postcode

Notice of Part Admission
(default action-fixed amount)

To the plaintiff(?s solicitor)

In the County Court	
Case Number *Always quote this*	
Plaintiff *(including ref.)*	
Defendant	

* *delete if no defence field*

Enclosed with this notice is a copy of the defendant?spart admission of your claim (Form N9A) (and a copy of the defendant?s part defence (Form N9A))*
- *Tick and complete either A or B and make sure that the judgment details at C are completed*
- *Remember to sign and date the form. Your signature certifies that the information you have given is correct.*

A ☐ I DO NOT accept the amount admitted by the defendant in the satisfaction of my claim

The court will arrange a date for a pre-trial review or the hearing of the action. You will be told when to come to court. If the case was not issued in the defendant?s local court, it will automatically be transferred there for the hearing. Where this case has been transferred to the defendant?s court, you may apply to that court in writing for the case to be transferred to a more convenient court. The district judge will consider your reasons on paper and there will be no need for you to attend court.

B ☐ I ACCEPT the amount admitted by the defendant in the satisfaction of my claim

Tick only **one** box below and follow the instructions given.

☐ **I accept the defendant?s proposal for payment**
Complete all the judgement details at C. The court will enter judgement in accordance with the offer and will send the defendant an order to pay. You will also be sent a copy.

☐ **The defendant has not made any proposal for payment**
Complete all the judgement details at C. Say how you want the defendant to pay. You can ask for the judgement to be paid by instalments or in one payment. The court will send the defendant an order to pay. You will also be sent a copy.

☐ **I do NOT accept the defendant?s proposal for payment**
Complete all the judgement details at C and say how you want the defendant to pay. Give your reasons for objecting to the defendant?s offer of payment in the space opposite. (Continue on the back of this form if necessary.) The court will fix a rate of payment and send the defendant an order to pay. You will also be sent a copy.

C Judgement details

If you are not accepting the defendant?s offer, say how you would like the judgement to be paid.

I would like the judgement to be paid

☐ (forthwith) *only tick this box if you intend to enforce the order right away*
☐ (by instalments of £ per month)
☐ (in full by)

Amount of claim as admitted (including interest at date of issue)..................	
Interest since date of summons (if any)..........	
Period........... Rate...........%	
Court fees (as applicable to part admission).....	
Solicitor?s costs (if any) on issuing summons	
Sub Total	
Solicitor?s costs (if any) on entering judgement	
Sub Total	
Deduct amount (if any) paid since issue..........	
Amount payable by defendant	

I certify that the information given is correct

Signed .... **Dated** ....

Appendix 3

Difference Between Small Claims Procedures in England & Wales and Scotland

Scotland	England and Wales
Administered by Sheriff Court	Administered by County Court
Limit of claim is £750 for small claims, £1,500 for summary cause procedure.	Limit of small claim is £3,000
Person against whom claim is made called the defender.	Person against whom claim is made called the defendant.
Person making claim known as the pursuer.	Person making claim known as the plaintiff.
Claims for payment of money completed on form 1. Claims for delivery or recovery of property completed on form 15. Claims for implementation of an obligation completed on form 18.	All claims lodged on form N1 Default Summons.
Claims between £750 and £1,500 dealt with under summary cause procedure.	Claims between £3,000 and £25,000 dealt with under normal County Court procedure.
Court fees: Small claims: Claims less than £50 Fee £5 Claims £50 to £750 Fee £19 Summary court pursuers fee: Claims £750 to £1,500 Fee £26	Court fees: (Examples of charges) Not more than £100 Fee £10 Not more than £600 Fee £60 Not more than £5,000 Fee £70 Over £5,000 Fee £80

Appendix 4

Glossary of Costing Terms

Absorbed Overhead	The overhead which, by means of rates of overhead absorption, is allotted to cost units.
Absorption Costing	The practice of charging all costs, both variable and fixed, to operations, processes or products.
Administration Cost	The cost of formulating the policy, directing the organisation and controlling the operations of an undertaking which is not related directly to a production, selling, distribution, research or development activity or function.
Batch	A cost unit which consists of a group of identical items which maintains its identity throughout one or more stages of production.
'Break-Even' Chart	A chart which shows profit or loss at various levels of activity, the level at which neither profit nor loss is shown being termed the break-even point. This may take the form of a chart on which is plotted the relationship either of total cost of sales to sales, or of fixed costs to contribution.
Budget Centre	A section of the organisation of an undertaking defined for the purposes of budgetary control.
Budgetary Control	The establishment of budgets relating the responsibilities of executives to the requirements of a policy and the continuous comparison of actual with budgeted results either to secure, by individual action, the objective of that policy or to provide a basis for its revision.

Calendar Volume
That portion of the volume variance which is due to the difference between the number of working days in the budget period and the number of working days in the period to which the budget is applied. (The sum of the calendar variances in a complete year would be zero.)

Note: This variance arises from the convention that fixed costs are the same for each period, whatever the number of working days, and it can be eliminated by apportioning standard allowances and actual fixed costs on a working day basis.

Capacity Usage Variance
That portion of the volume variance which is due to working at higher or lower capacity usage than standard.

Contribution
The difference between sales value and the marginal cost of sales.

Controllable Cost
A cost which can be influenced by the action of a specified member of an undertaking.

Controllable Cost Variance
A cost variance which can be identified as the primary responsibility of a specified person.

Cost
(i) The amount of expenditure (actual or notional) incurred on, or attributable to, a given thing.
(ii) To ascertain the cost of a given thing.

Note: The word 'cost' can rarely stand on its own and should be quantified as to its nature or limitations (eg historical, variable etc) and related to a particular thing or 'object of thought' (eg a given quantity or unit of goods made or services provided.

Cost Accountancy
The application of costing and cost accounting principles, methods and techniques to the science, art and practice of

cost control and the ascertainment of profitability. It includes the presentation of information derived from it for the purpose of managerial decision making.

Cost Accounting

The process of accounting for cost from the point at which expenditure is incurred or committed to the establishment of its ultimate relationship with cost centres and cost units. In its widest usage, it embraces the preparation of statistical data, the application of cost control methods and the ascertainment of the profitability of activities carried out or planned.

Cost Allocation

The allotment of whole items of cost to cost centres or cost units.

Cost Apportionment

The allotment of proportions of items of cost to cost centres or cost units.

Note: The words 'allocation', 'apportionment' and 'allotment' will be found in some text books to have exactly the same meaning. The distinction made in the above two definitions implies a greater degree of precision to 'allocation'. Thus one allocates direct expenditure which can be directly identified with a cost centre or cost unit but one apportions indirect expenditure.

Cost Centre

A location, person or item of equipment (or group of these) for which costs may be ascertained and used for the purposes of cost control.

Cost Classification

(i) The process of grouping costs according to their common characteristics.
(ii) A series of specified groups according to which costs are classified.

Cost Code A series of alphabetical and/or numerical symbols, each of which represents a descriptive title in a cost classification.

Cost Estimate Sheet A document which provides for the assembly of the estimated detailed cost in respect of a cost centre or cost unit.

Cost Unit A unit of quantity of product, service or time (or a combination of these) in relation to which costs may be ascertained or expressed.

Cost Variance The difference between a standard cost and the comparable actual cost incurred during a period.

Cost of Sales The cost which is attributable to the sales made.

Note: It is not uncommon to use this in a restricted sense as the production cost of goods sold.

Costing The techniques and processes of ascertaining costs.

Depreciation The dimunition in the value of a fixed asset due to use and/or the lapse of time.

Note: Conventional methods of calculating depreciation, which usually take into account the assumed life of the asset and any residual value, are given later. See also Obsolescence.

Development Cost The cost of the process which begins with the implementation of the decision to produce a new or improved product or to employ a new or improved method and ends with the commencement of formal production of that product or by that method.

Direct Costing	The practice of charging all direct costs to operations, processes or products, leaving all indirect costs to be written off against profits in the period in which they arise. **Note:** This differs from marginal costing in that some fixed costs could be considered to be direct costs in appropriate circumstances.
Direct Expenses	Expenses which can be identified with, and allocated to, cost centres or cost units.
Direct Labour Efficiency Variance	That portion of the direct wages variance which is due to the difference between the standard labour hours specified for the activity achieved and the actual labour hours expended. **Note:** Where efficiency is measured by a line speed or cost centre output as distinct from the output of an individual worker, it may be possible to sub-analyse this variance between efficiency and amount of direct labour usage.
Direct Materials Cost	Materials cost which can be identified with, and allocated to, cost centres or cost units.
Direct Materials Cost Variance	The difference between the standard cost of direct materials specified for the output achieved and the actual cost of direct materials used.
Direct Materials Mixture Variance	That portion of the direct materials usage variance which is due to the difference between the standard and actual composition of a mixture. (Applicable only when direct materials are physically mixed.)
Direct Materials Price Variance	That portion of the direct materials cost variance which is due to the difference between the standard price specified and the actual price paid.

Direct Materials Usage Variance — That portion of the direct materials cost variance which is due to the difference between the standard quantity specified and the actual quantity used.

Direct Materials Yield Variance — That portion of the direct materials usage variance which is due to the difference between the standard yield specified and the actual yield obtained.

Direct Wages (Direct Labour Costs) — Wages (Labour Cost) which can be identified with, and allocated to, cost centres or cost units.

Direct Wages Rate Variance — That portion of the direct wages variance which is due to the difference between the standard rate of pay specified and the actual rate paid.

Direct Wages Variance — The difference between the standard direct wages specified for the activity achieved and the actual direct wages paid.

Distribution Cost — The cost of the sequence of operations which begins with making the packaged product available for despatch and ends with making the reconditioned returned empty package, if any, available for re-use.

Note: As well as including expenditure incurred in transporting articles to central or local storage, distribution cost includes expenditure incurred in moving articles to and from prospective customers as in the case of goods on 'sale or return' basis. In the gas, electricity and water industries, 'distribution' means pipes, mains and services which may be regarded as the equivalent of packing and transportation

Expenses — The cost of services provided to an undertaking and the notional cost of the use of owned assets.

First In First Out Price (FIFO)
: The price paid for the material first taken into the stock from which the materials to be priced could have been drawn.

Fixed Budget
: A budget which is designed to remain unchanged irrespective of the level of activity actually attained.

Fixed Cost
: A cost which tends to be unaffected by variations in volume of output. Fixed costs depend mainly on the efflux of time and do not vary directly with volume or rate of output. Fixed costs are sometimes referred to as period costs in systems of direct costing.

Note: There may be different levels of fixed costs at different levels of output, eg where extra output is only obtainable by extra capital equipment or extra services. At the other extreme, when a whole department may be shut down, many of these costs will, in fact, disappear.

Flexible Budget
: A budget which, by recognising the difference between fixed, semi-fixed and variable costs, is designed to change in relation to the level of activity attained.

Historical Costing
: The ascertainment of costs after they have been incurred.

Impersonal Cost Centre
: A cost centre which consists of a location or item of equipment (or group of these).

Indirect Expenses
: Expenses which cannot be allocated but which can be apportioned to, or absorbed by, cost centres or cost units.

Indirect Materials Cost
: Materials cost which cannot be allocated but which can be apportioned to, or absorbed by, cost centres or cost units.

Indirect Wages (Indirect Labour Cost)
: Wages (Labour Cost) which cannot be allocated but which can be apportioned to, or absorbed by, cost centres or cost units.

Integrated Accounts A system in which the financial and cost accounts are interlocked to ensure that all relevant expenditure is absorbed into the cost accounts.

Inventory A schedule of items held at a particular point in time.

Note: The American usage of the term is synonymous with our use of 'stocks', including consumable materials, work-in-progress and finished goods.

Job A cost unit which consists of a single order (or contract).

Last In First Out Price (LIFO) The price paid for the material last taken into the stock from which the material to be priced could have been drawn.

Marginal Cost The amount of any given volume of output by which aggregate costs are changed if the volume of output is increased or decreased by one unit. In practice, this is measured by the total variable cost attributable to one unit.

Note: In this context, a unit may be a single article, a batch of articles, an order, a stage of production capacity, a process or a department. It relates to the change in output in the particular circumstances under consideration.

Marginal Costing The ascertainment of marginal costs and of the effect on profit of changes in volume or type of output by differentiating between fixed costs and variable costs.

Note: In this method of costing, only variable costs are charged to operations, processes or products while fixed costs are written off against profits in the period in which they arise.

Materials Cost The cost of commodities supplied to an undertaking.

Methods Variance The difference between the standard cost of a product or operation produced or performed by the normal method and the standard cost of the product or operation produced or performed by the alternative method actually employed.

Operating Statement A summary of the operating costs (and, where appropriate, of the income and margins) of the whole or part of the activities of an undertaking for a given period.

Note: In budgetary control and standard costing systems, operating statements will usually provide information regarding the units produced in the period, the comparison of actual and standard or budgeted costs, income and margins and an analysis of the variances.

Operation Cost Centre A cost centre which consists of those machines and/or persons carrying out similar operations.

Overhead The aggregate of indirect materials cost, indirect wages (indirect labour cost) and indirect expenses.

Note: 'Oncost' and 'burden' are synonymous terms which are not recommended.

Overhead Absorption The allotment of overhead to cost units.

Note: Overhead absorption is usually achieved by the use of one, or a combination of, overhead rates. Such rates are often referred to as 'recovery' rates. The use of this term is somewhat confusing since it may be understood to imply ultimate recovery in selling price, which is not necessarily achieved, and, for this reason, 'absorption' is recommended.

Overhead Efficiency Variance That portion of the overhead expenditure variance which is the difference between the standard allowance for the

activity (standard hours achieved) and the standard allowance for the actual hours worked.
Note: This variance only arises on costs which vary with time taken rather than with volume of output.

Overhead Expenditure Variance That portion of the overhead variance which represents the difference between the standard allowance for the output achieved and the actual expenditure incurred.

Overhead Price Variance That portion of the overhead variance which is due to the difference between the standard price of the service specified and the actual price paid.

Overhead Rate The expression of overhead in relation to some specific characteristic of a cost centre as a means of providing a convenient basis for its apportionment or absorption.

Note: Such rates may include:
- percentage rates based upon direct wages
- direct materials cost
- prime cost
- rates per machine hour
- rates per labour hour
- rates per cost unit etc.

Overhead Utilisation Variance That portion of the overhead expenditure variance which is due to the difference between the standard quantity of the service specified and the actual quantity of the service used.

Overhead Variance The difference between the standard cost of overhead absorbed in the output achieved and the actual overhead cost.

Perpetual Inventory A system of records maintained by the controlling department which reflects the physical movement of stocks and their current balance.

Personal Cost Centre A cost centre which consists of a person or group of persons.

Predetermined Cost A cost which is computed in advance of production on the basis of a specification of all the factors affecting cost.

Pre-Production Cost That part of development cost incurred in making a trial production run preliminary to formal production.

Note: This term is sometimes used to cover all activities prior to production including research and development but, in such cases, the usage should be made clear in the context.

Prime Cost The aggregate of direct materials cost, direct wages (direct labour cost) and variable direct expenses.

Process Cost Centre A cost centre which consists of a specific process or a continuous sequence of operations.

Product Group A cost unit which consists of a group of similar products.

Production Cost The cost of the sequence of operations which begins with supplying materials, labour and services and ends with primary packing of the product.

Replacement Price The price at which there could be purchased an asset identical to that which is being replaced or revalued.

Research Cost The cost of searching for new or improved products, new applications of materials or new, or improved, methods.

Revision Variance The variance between the basic standard cost and the revised standard cost.

Seasonal Variance That portion of the volume variance which is due to the difference between the seasonally-budgeted output and the average output on which standards have been calculated.

(The sum of the seasonal variations over a complete year would be zero.)

Selling Cost The cost of seeking to create and stimulate demand (sometimes termed 'marketing') and of securing orders.

Semi-Fixed Cost A cost which is partly fixed and partly variable.

Semi-Variable Cost See semi-fixed cost.

Simple Average Price A price which is calculated by dividing the total of the prices of the materials in the stock from which the material to be priced could be drawn by the number of prices used in that total.

Standard Cost A predetermined cost which is calculated from management's standards of efficient operation and the relevant necessary expenditure. It may be used as a basis for price-fixing and for cost control through variance analysis.

Standard Costing The preparation and use of standard costs, their comparison with actual costs and the analysis of variances to their causes and points of incidence.

Standard Price A predetermined price fixed on the basis of a specification of all the factors affecting that price.

Total Cost The sum of all costs attributable to the unit under consideration.

Note: This term should always be qualified as it can mean the total cost of an undertaking or it can mean the total cost attributed to a process or to a product or to a service.

Total Cost Variance The difference between the total standard cost value of the output achieved in a period and the total actual cost incurred.

Under or Over-Absorbed Overhead The difference between the amount of overhead absorbed and the amount of overhead incurred.

Uniform Costing The use by several undertakings of the same costing principles and/or practices.

Variable Cost A cost which tends to vary directly with volume of output. Variable costs are sometimes referred to as direct costs in systems of direct costing.

Variance Ratio The resolution into constituent parts and the explanation of variances.

Volume Efficiency Variance That portion of the volume variance which reflects the increased or reduced output arising from efficiency above or below the standard which is expected.

Volume Variance That portion of the overhead variance which is the difference between the standard cost of overhead absorbed in actual output and the standard allowance for that output. (This represents the over or under-absorption of fixed costs in the period concerned.)

Wages (Labour Cost) The costs of remuneration (wages, salaries, commissions, bonuses etc) of the employees of an undertaking.

Weighted Average Price A price which is calculated by dividing the total cost of materials in the stock from which the material to be priced could be drawn by the total quantity of materials in that stock.

Index